KNOWING AND
TEACHING THE
MIGRANT CHILD

ELIZABETH SUTTON

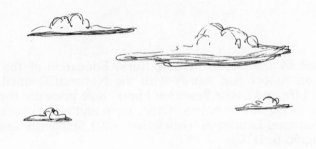

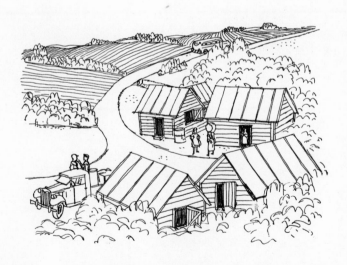

Copyright 1960
National Education Association of the United States
Department of Rural Education
Library of Congress Catalog Card Number: 60-16936

Published by the Department of Rural Education of the National
Education Association jointly with the National Council on Agri-
cultural Life and Labor Research Fund. Sale price per copy, $3.50.
Discounts on quantity orders. Order from and make checks payable
to the National Education Association, 1201 Sixteenth Street, N.W.,
Washington 6, D. C.

Foreword

The American goal of an adequate opportunity for each child to receive education commensurate with his capabilities is an ideal more nearly achieved in some sections of our society than others. One group for which the goal remains remote is made up of children whose parents move about the country in order to perform seasonal work in industrial agriculture. This book is an outgrowth of a special project conducted in two counties—one in Virginia and one in Florida—on the education of the children of agricultural migratory workers.

Since the writer was so closely associated with every aspect of the Project, the book lays no claim to objectivity. It is a report of the practices followed and the conclusions reached by the Supervisor and the teachers with whom she worked, with special attention to the means of knowing the migrant child and of adapting school procedures to his needs.

The agricultural migratory movement and the problems of education it creates are not limited to any one area, but are of concern throughout the country. Though the firsthand experiences of the writer were limited to contact with the agricultural workers and their children of the Eastern seaboard migratory stream as she followed them from Florida to and from Virginia, she corresponded with schools all over the United States who had migrants enrolled. The families with whom the writer worked had been in as many as 44 states.

As plans for publishing the results of the Project were developed, it became evident that there were two audiences to be served. One audience is composed of public-school personnel—teachers, supervisors, curriculum workers, administrators—who are or may be employed in school systems that serve migratory children and teacher-preparation institutions which have responsibility for the preservice and inservice education of public-school personnel. The other audience is limited to the people who would be concerned with the planning and administrative details of the Project—

national and community agencies, organizations, and groups who work for the improvement of communities in which agricultural migratory workers and their families reside. The present volume is addressed to the first audience. A second volume is being made available on a more limited basis.

HOWARD A. DAWSON
Executive Secretary
Department of Rural Education, NEA

CONTENTS

Acknowledgments

It is impossible to give credit to the many people whose ideas and experiences were embodied in the conduct of the Project and in the preparation of this report. However, the writer wishes to acknowledge and extend sincere appreciation to the following organizations, groups, and individuals who made major contributions:

The Migrant Research Fund and the Executive Board of the National Council on Agricultural Life and Labor (see Appendix I, p. 131), who conceived and initiated the plan of the Project, who arranged the financial assistance, and who gave loyal support and encouragement to the Project Supervisor.

In Florida, the Palm Beach County Board of Public Instruction, West Palm Beach; Howell L. Watkins, Superintendent of Public Instruction, and Mrs. Clara Hunter Capron, Director of Instruction, Palm Beach County Schools; the supervisors of Palm Beach, who worked cooperatively with the Project Supervisor and the advisory committees; Wilbur Marshall, General Consultant, who served as liaison to the Project from the State Department of Education of Florida; the General Extension Division of the University of Florida, Gainesville; the School of Education, Florida State University; and the Agricultural and Mechanical University in Tallahassee, who arranged and conducted extension classes in the Glades area of Palm Beach County.

In Virginia, the Northampton County School Board, Eastville; William F. Lawson, Jr., Division Superintendent, Northampton County Schools; the supervisors of Northampton County, who worked cooperatively with the Project Supervisor and the advisory committee; and Tom V. Downing, Assistant Supervisor of Vocational Education, who served as liaison to the Project from the State Department of Education in Virginia.

For help in both counties, special credit is due the classroom teachers, attendance workers, special education teachers, and principals who were involved in the Project, who worked directly with migrant children and who, in an effort to extend and improve edu-

vi

cational opportunities for these children, furnished the greater part of the data and information on which this report is based; the advisory committees who gave direction to all aspects of the Project; the Department of Rural Education of the National Education Association and the United States Office of Education who, from time to time, provided consultative services to the Project; and the national voluntary organizations and governmental agencies who provided information on migrants (see Appendix I and II, p. 131-133).

In addition, the writer is especially indebted to the following for help during the writing of the report:

H. A. Curtis, Head of the Department of Educational Research and Testing, School of Education, Florida State University, who has given exceptionally valuable suggestions and criticism during the writing of the entire report.

Lois M. Clark, Assistant Director of the Department of Rural Education, National Education Association, who gave many valuable suggestions on the original manuscript and who has assisted in the editing of the final manuscript.

Mrs. Ruth S. Irvin, Principal of the Osceola School, Belle Glade, Florida, who assisted the writer in the analysis of the data and the development of the original manuscript of Chapter III, and who has given valuable suggestions on other sections of the report.

Howard A. Dawson, Executive Director of Rural Service, National Education Association, who continually has given guidance and encouragement to the writer, and who has manifested genuine interest in all aspects of the Project and the development of the report.

The Publications Division of the National Education Association for production of the book, especially, Robert L. Thompson, assistant director; Mrs. Janet Leban, copy editor; and Thomas Gladden, staff artist.

ELIZABETH SUTTON

Tallahassee, Florida
July 1960

The Project

In 1951, the National Council on Agricultural Life and Labor[1] and six of its member organizations whose work is related to the education and welfare of children created a seven-member Migrant Research Project Board[2] consisting of one representative from each of the organizations. The purpose of the Board was to sponsor a research project designed to provide a factual, objective basis for plans and programs to improve the educational opportunities and experiences of the children of agricultural migratory workers.[3]

At this stage of the Project, effort was centered on a series of localized case studies representing various streams of migratory movement. Nineteen state superintendents of public instruction in states known to employ agricultural migratory workers were approached as to their interest in cooperating with such a study. Of the 16 states replying favorably, Florida, Virginia, Texas, and Illinois were selected as best representing all aspects of the problem. With the further advice and counsel of each state superintendent, four areas were selected for study: the Glades area, Palm Beach County, Florida; Northampton County, Virginia; the Seguin Independent School District, Guadalupe County, Texas; and the Hoopeston-Milford-Rossville School Districts, Vermilion and Iroquois counties, Illinois.

The Research Project extended from July 1, 1952, to December 31, 1953. Procedures used in securing research data and in field contacts, as well as the findings of the Project, are reported by the Project Director, the Rev. Shirley E. Greene, in *The Education of Migrant Children*.[4]

---

[1] The nature of the composition and concerns of the National Council on Agricultural Life and Labor are presented in Appendix I, p. 131.

[2] The names of the cosponsoring agencies are listed in Appendix I, p. 131.

[3] Prior to this Project, increasing concern for the educational needs of agricultural migratory children had been expressed by numerous local and national organizations and by departments of the U.S. Government.

[4] Greene, Shirley E. *The Education of Migrant Children*. Washington, D. C.: Department of Rural Education, National Education Association, 1954.

1

INITIAL PLANS FOR THE PROJECT

As a result of this exploratory work, decision was made by the Migrant Research Project Board to undertake a demonstration Pilot Project, experimental in nature, in cooperation with the school authorities in Palm Beach County, Florida, and Northampton County, Virginia, to capitalize on the findings of the Research Project and to develop ways of implementing its recommendations.

To carry out this decision a Memorandum of Agreement, outlining the duties and responsibilities of each of the parties, was drawn up by the National Council on Agricultural Life and Labor, through the Migrant Research Project Board, the Board of Public Instruction of Palm Beach County, Florida, and the Northampton County School Board, Virginia, and approved by the Florida and Virginia state departments of education. The state departments of education pledged their cooperation and each designated a person on their staff to serve as liaison to the Pilot Project, which was inaugurated on July 1, 1954, to continue through June 30, 1957.

The central feature of the Pilot Project involved the employment jointly by the two county school systems, with the financial assistance of the NCALL Migrant Research Fund,[5] of the writer of this book as a supervisory specialist in migrant education. The Supervisor was employed as a regular member of the headquarters staff of each of the counties to work under the direction of the county superintendent, to whom she was responsible in her day-to-day work. Her time was to be divided between the two counties on a schedule corresponding to the agricultural migratory movement. Each of the county school systems was to furnish the Supervisor with office space, equipment, and secretarial assistance.

The Pilot Project was experimental in nature, and therefore an outline of work was somewhat flexible. Originally, however, plans included:

1. Use of experiments in the education of migratory children through a study of existing literature and through personal contacts

2. Work on enrollment and attendance problems, which would involve cooperation with attendance officers, parents, crew leaders, growers, employment service officials, and others, aimed at securing the enrollment of migrant children on the

[5] For purposes of this Pilot Project the Migrant Research Project Board was enlarged by the addition of representatives of the Alliance for the Guidance of Rural Youth and the National Sharecroppers Fund and by a consultant from the United States Office of Education. Later the Migrant Research Project Board became the Migrant Research Fund of the NCALL.

earliest possible date and their regular attendance at school throughout the period of their residence in the community

3. Experimentation with and work on problems of curriculum adaptation which would involve the identification of specific needs of migratory children, and a careful study of school practices in terms of possible modifications

4. Development of techniques for record transfers from school to school

5. Interpretation of the problems and possibilities in the education of agricultural migratory children to the general public.

As the Project developed, advisory committees and extension classes were held and a helping teacher program was begun.

The advisory committees, in both Northampton and Palm Beach counties, were established to give direction to all phases of the Project. In both counties, the committees developed an experimental transfer record for migrant children and a letter of welcome to their parents. In Northampton County the committee initiated the helping teacher program and in Palm Beach County they sponsored extension classes from Florida State University and Florida Agricultural and Mechanical University in Tallahassee.

The helping teacher program, discussed in detail in Chapter 6, was begun to meet the need for additional teachers created by the influx of migrant children into the schools.

Extension courses were held to explore better ways of working with classes in which migratory children were enrolled. Classes, for undergraduate or graduate credit, were held on a workshop basis. Areas for study included understanding the migrant family, welcoming and accepting migrants into school, using people and agencies in the community for help, and developing instructional materials and improving methods of instruction in classes attended by migrants.[6]

SOURCES FOR DATA

From the beginning, records were kept so that a report could be prepared at the conclusion of the Project. This book is based on a

---

[6] Two reports made at the conclusion of the courses are available for use in working with migrant children:

Florida Agricultural and Mechanical University. *A Guide to the Education of Agricultural Migratory Children.* Tallahassee: the University (Edwin F. Norwood, Director of Extension Services), 1956. (Mimeographed)

Florida State University. *Working with Migrant Children in Our Schools.* Tallahassee: the University (H. A. Curtis, School of Education), 1956. (Mimeographed)

careful' analysis of data obtained from:

1. A daily journal kept by the Supervisor throughout the Project in which she recorded her activities; personal conferences with migrant parents, children, school personnel, and other persons in the communities; and interpretations she made of these observations as she became familiar with general conditions

2. Approximately 300 descriptions, submitted by teachers during the final year of the Project, of "practices that seemed to make a real difference in the adjustment and learning of migrant children." Analysis of these revealed more than 1200 school practices, the great majority of which were judged successful by the teachers

3. Approximately 2000 compositions by children, written under guidance of classroom teachers, on such topics as, "Why I Like (or Do Not Like) To Travel," "The School I Have Liked the Best (or Least) and Why," "The Teacher I Have Liked the Best (or Least) and Why," "How I Feel When I Move," and "How I Feel When I Go to a New School"

4. Memorandums kept on each meeting of the advisory committees in both areas

5. Three bulletins developed during the Project, two reports of the extension classes held in Palm Beach County—"A Guide to the Teaching of Agricultural Migratory Children" and "Working with Migrant Children in Our Schools"—and a report of the helping teacher program in Northampton County—"A Guide to the Teaching of Reading."

Though no standard definition of a "migrant child" exists that is accepted by all workers and agencies in the field of migrant education, the term, as defined and used during the Project and in the book, refers to a child whose family, within the past twelve months, has moved at least once across a county or state line for the purpose of seeking or engaging in agricultural labor.

THE EXPERIMENTAL AREAS

The two areas in which the Pilot Project was carried out were selected in order to demonstrate two important aspects of the migrant problem: the Palm Beach County "home-base" area where the migrants spend a relatively longer period of time and Northampton County, the "on-the-trek" situation, visited by the migrant group on northward trips in the spring and early summer and on southward trips in the late summer and early fall.

The Glades

The Glades area lies in the extreme western portion of Palm Beach County, Florida. The area borders Lake Okeechobee, the second largest fresh-water lake in the United States, and is separated from the coastal area by a wide belt of recently developed swamplands, which accounts for two-thirds of the one and a quarter million acres of land in Palm Beach County.

Until about 1920, when the first serious attempt at developing an agricultural economy was made in the area, the Glades was known only for its wastelands and Indian lore. Since that time, the area has risen in national prominence as the world's largest winter vegetable-producing empire and the nation's largest sugar cane-producing area. The Glades is known also for its cattle and ramie industries.

The rich black muck soil of the area, which lies from six to eight feet deep, contains about 75 percent, and sometimes as much as 90 percent, organic matter. The people of the Glades proudly refer to this soil as "Black Gold."

The farmlands of the region are flat and water control is accomplished through a system of canals, ditches, and pumps. This standard land-water system is used reversibly as the season demands, either to drain water off or pump it on to the land. Usually the area has a frost-free climate which averages 79 degrees in summer and 70 degrees in winter, and the average annual temperature is 74.7 degrees. Average annual rainfall is 55 inches. The subtropical climate and productivity of the soil make growth rapid. Three, four, and sometimes as many as eight crops are produced on the same land during one season.

The combination of the Glades soil, climate, tenure pattern, and cropping pattern, as well as continuous experimentation with development of crops, has created an industrialized agriculture characterized by large units of ownership, large capital investment, professional management, and the employment of very large contingents of seasonal wage labor.

The harvest season extends for a period of six to seven months. At the beginning of November, vegetables begin to move in volume, and harvesting operations continue, shifting from crop to crop, into May. Within this time there are peaks and troughs of labor demand. The Belle Glade office of the State Employment Service provides information on the numbers of agricultural laborers required in the area monthly to grow and harvest crops. During the Project the following estimates were made: October—7672; November—13,767; December—12,843; January—9643; February—

10,996; March—11,983; April—15,624; May—8127; June—4636; July—2068; August—2006; September—3101.

Five farm labor camps—three Negro and two white—are located in the Glades. These camps provide living accommodations for approximately 1600 family units. Built by the Federal Farm Security Administration between 1939 and 1942, they have been owned and operated by local housing authorities since 1947. Many of the larger homes in these camps are occupied now by permanent residents, and their availability has been a major factor in stabilizing a portion of the formerly seasonal population.

The rapidly expanding agricultural enterprises and the phenomenal growth of the Glades reflect the progressive attitudes of its citizens. A frontier atmosphere permeates the area and the citizens are quick to promote new programs, experimentation, and research. Coupled with this tendency toward inquiry and action is a humanitarian concern for the migrants, who, though temporary, are vital members of the community.

The schools of the Glades are a part of a large county school system which offers many services beyond the usual standard public-school education. Administratively, the levels are elementary, grades 1-6; junior high, grades 7-9; senior high, grades 10-12; and Palm Beach Junior College, grades 13 and 14. An increasing number of citizens are served through the adult education and vocational education programs. Increasing population throughout the county has affected the school system, which is undergoing rapid growth and change—building programs, expanded facilities, and additional personnel on administrative, supervisory, and teaching staffs.

Conforming to the Florida state school laws, schools are administered by a county superintendent of public instruction who is popularly elected for a term of four years. The County Board of Public Instruction is composed of five members who are elected by county-wide vote for a term of two years, one from each of the five county board membership districts. Two members of this board are from the Glades area. In addition, there are three school trustees, elected by popular vote for two years from three different residence districts, who serve primarily as an advisory and limited policy-forming body for the county schools. One of these trustees represents the Glades area.

Serving all schools and operating from the county office in West Palm Beach are a number of professional personnel whose assignments cover matters of curriculum and supervision of instruction— elementary and secondary, guidance program for exceptional children, adult and vocational education, personnel, school lunch,

school finance, maintenance of school plants, textbooks and supplies, transportation, and attendance.

The county school system operates six white schools and seven
Negro schools in the Glades area. These schools make up approximately 14 percent and 32 percent, respectively, of the number of
schools in the county. Enrollment in these schools fluctuates from
the continual entrance and withdrawal of large numbers of transient children. All schools experience considerable increases in
enrollment between the beginning weeks of a school term and the
mid term. To accommodate these peak enrollments, an additional
number of teachers are employed at the opening of the school year,
and some extra teachers are supplied later. Usually, the classroom
teaching loads are very light the first few weeks of the school term.

Northampton County

Northampton County, 950 miles from the Glades, is the south-
ernmost of the two counties which lie at the southern tip of the
Delmarva Peninsula and constitute the eastern shore of Virginia.
The county is long and very narrow, with an average width of about
six miles, and is bounded on the east by the Atlantic Ocean and
on the west by the Chesapeake Bay. Inlets from the ocean and
the bay extending several miles inland in a winding fashion make
the extensive water frontage of the county very irregular.

Historically, Northampton County is one of the most interesting
counties in the United States. The earliest English exploration of
this area was made by Captain John Smith in 1608, and the first
settlement was about 1614. Today, Northampton and Accomack
counties occupy the area which was one of the original eight Virginia shires of 1634. The entire eastern shore bore the name
Accomack until 1642, when the county was renamed Northampton
after an old English county, and in 1663 the two present counties
were formed. Eastville, the county seat, has the oldest continuous
court records in America. Throughout the county numerous ances-
tral homes, built from 1700 to 1825, are still standing. Many of
them, furnished with antiques of the eighteenth century, and surrounded by flower gardens, shrubbery, and trees, reflect the gra-
cious living of colonial America.

In 1950, Northampton County had a population of approximately
18,000, with about 5000 living in the four incorporated towns, Cape
Charles, Cheriton, Eastville, and Exmore. The county is closely
linked by U.S. Highway No. 13, which runs the full length of the
county and is a part of the coastal highway serving the Maine to
Florida traffic. Passage across Chesapeake Bay is by ferry steam-

ers operating between Kiptopeke Beach, the world's largest ferry terminal, and Little Creek in Princess Anne County to the south.

The economy of the county is derived primarily from vegetable and truck farming. Because of its geographical location, the area enjoys the benefits of a moderate climate. The mean temperature is 59.7 degrees. The annual rainfall ranges between 40 and 45 inches. On the average, there are 222 frost-free days each year. The productive sandy loam soil, aided by this long growing season and mild climate, permits intensive cultivation to the extent of two and sometimes three regular crops a year.

Agricultural enterprises in Northampton County are family farms relatively small in size, the chief source of income for the owner and his family. Farm operations are supplemented by special labor during peak seasons. Seasonal labor demands usually expand during the period from the beginning of May through the middle of July, and again during the months of September and October. To meet this need, approximately 6000 migratory laborers (a number which has been fairly constant for the past 15 years) are recruited from Florida and the Southeastern states. The great majority of these migrant laborers are Negroes, who are transported by crew leaders in groups ranging in size from 50 to 300. An increasing number of workers are Texas-Mexicans, some are Puerto Ricans, and relatively few are Anglo-whites. These groups usually travel in family units. Generally, the pattern of migration is as follows: Workers begin to arrive the latter part of April, reach peak numbers in June and July, and after the first of August move northward along the Atlantic seaboard into New York, New Jersey, and often as far as Maine. Many of these same migratory workers come back to Northampton County for the fall harvest, arriving about the middle of September and remaining six to eight weeks before moving south by the beginning of November.

Virginia operates its public-school system through a series of school divisions. Northampton County represents a single and separate school division which includes all of the public county schools and the schools operated by the independent school district of Cape Charles. Conforming to the Virginia school division system, the Northampton school division is administered by a superintendent who is appointed for a term of four years. His appointment is made by the local County Board of Education, who make their selection from an approved list submitted by the State Department of Education. This list also is approved by the State Board of Education before it is submitted to the County Board. The County Board of Education is composed of four members, three of whom are appointed by the School Trustee Electoral Board. This Electoral Board is appointed by the Judge of the State Circuit Court. The School Board of the Cape Charles Special School District is composed of three members appointed by the Town Council of Cape Charles, and the Chairman of this Board is a member of the County School Board. All members of both school boards serve for a term of four years.

The office of the Northampton Division School Board is located at Eastville. The Division Superintendent, the Supervisor of the white schools, and the Supervisor of the Negro schools serve all schools from this office. No school attendance personnel is employed. All schools draw heavily on the services of both the local health and welfare departments.

Operating in the school division are eight county schools—four Negro and four white. Grades one through seven are taught in each of the elementary schools, and grades eight through twelve in each of the two high schools.

The number of school-age migratory children who enter this area is not known since the peak harvesting seasons occur during the closing weeks of school—from the middle of April through May—and during the opening months of school—September and October. Information from the local office of the Virginia Employment Service presents the best picture of the number of migratory children who enter the area. From April 1 through May 30, 1956, but mainly from the beginning to the middle of May, 262 children under the age of 14 moved into the area: 123 Mexicans, 116 Negroes, and 23 Puerto Ricans. From April 1 through May 30, 1957, there were 350 children: 2 Anglo-whites, 153 Negroes, 149 Mexicans, and 46 Puerto Ricans. Of this number, 150 entered from May 1 through May 5. These figures, it should be noted, included all children under 14 years of age, and it is very likely that practically half were under school age. Estimates of the number of school-age migratory children who reside in the county sometime between April and November range from 500 to 550.

THE SUPERVISOR BEGINS WORK

As she began her work with the Project the Supervisor knew the results of the findings and recommendations of the research study and her responsibility as identified in the Memorandum of Agreement. However, she realized that the Pilot Project would develop, to a great extent, in terms of her relationships with the personnel of the two school systems, as a regular member of the supervisory staffs and as a supervisor assigned to the special responsibility for improving and extending the educational opportunities of migratory children; with community agencies and organizations serving migratory families; with local, regional, state, and national lay and professional groups as a representative of migrant education; and with individuals who exercise natural leadership as well as with those who hold positional leadership. She must develop these relationships, she believed, in terms of her own philosophy and convictions as to the effective ways of working with people.

The Supervisor soon became aware of certain factors in the life pattern of the migratory child:

1. His life is not related to community living in the usual ways
2. He must make repeated adjustments to new school situations, with frustrations resulting from the inadequacies of his background
3. He faces a community situation where there is little awareness of his needs and little understanding of the contribution his family makes to the community's economic development
4. His family lacks appreciation of the value of education, the need for proper housing and sanitation, good health habits, child care, and the value of budgeting money
5. His parents usually are nonvoters who lack understanding of the resources and services normally available to American citizens through governmental or private agencies.

As the Supervisor worked with teachers and principals in the preschool planning periods in the two school systems, they identified five problem areas:

1. Problems related to the home life of the child
2. Problems related to home-school relationships
3. Problems related to school records and transfers
4. Problems related to curriculum and organization for instruction
5. Problems related to materials for instruction.

Succeeding chapters take up the problems of the migrant child in detail, his life and his schooling, and the methods developed during the Project to meet, and attempt to solve, these problems.

How they live

Wherever the production of seasonal crops requires hand labor, migratory workers "move with the crops." Their existence is essential to an agricultural economy which requires that workers be available at a precise moment in order to plant, cultivate, harvest, or process the crops and send them on the way to national markets. These migrants work in what is usually the only type of labor open to them. They have no permanent homes; they are poorly clothed and nourished. Inadequate wages trap them in a cycle of seasonal migration difficult to break.

The migratory stream on the Eastern seaboard, which originates in Florida and moves northward and westward, is made up of Negroes and whites, with an increasing number of Americans of Mexican extraction from southern Texas and some Puerto Ricans. Many agricultural migrants are displaced sharecroppers or small farmers. Handicapped in finding regular jobs because they lack sufficient education or special skills, they travel in search of agricultural jobs until they can find some better way of making a living. Some are people from urban areas who have been thrown out of work by industrial change or adjustment. Still others may own small farms and migrate during slack seasons to supplement their meager incomes and to look around for a more desirable living situation.

The children of the workers suffer the greatest damage from a migratory existence. They are learning the way of life of their group and are coming to accept the goals and expectations of their parents. They share, in common, mobility and its limitations, among them the limited opportunities open to them for getting an education and of using the knowledge to gain a better way of life. Should a child attend school, every time he moves he faces an adjustment to a new school situation, with frustrations resulting from the inadequacies of his background. The entire situation is intensified by two facts, that the children's parents have little desire for them to attend school and that many communities do not

13

expect or may discourage them from going to school for the short
time they are resident. Only in communities where people become
sensitive to the deprivations in the lives of migrant children are
broadened and enriched educational opportunities made available
to them.

THE MOBILE LIFE OF THE MIGRANT CHILD

The migrant child lives for short periods of time during each year
in several communities, sometimes in two, four, six, and even eight
different states. Even though his family may have a well-estab-
lished migratory route, there is no assurance that, while on the
trek, he will reside in the same communities year after year.

To some migrant children home is the location where they live
the longest time during a year, usually where the family resides
during the winter, or where they visit a grandparent or relative for
a few weeks during the slack seasons. To others, home has no
meaning whatsoever, and in response to questions regarding it,
they answer, "Nope, ain't got no home. Just any place we're at,
that's my home" or "I don't know, you see we just move a lot."

Some children, whose parents have established a somewhat
regular pattern of migration, live in only two or three states during
a year and return each fall to the same area. This does not mean,
however, that the child enrolls in the same school in each area every
year. Annually, he may move into the same state, and even the
same county, but his parents may work for a different grower and
live in a different community, and the child will attend a different
school.

While on the trek, there is no definitely scheduled time in any
location. Length of stay is determined by the weather, the supply
of adequate labor, the crops to be harvested, and the availability
of housing. During some seasons, the child may live in a community for only a few days or weeks, for as long as four months or, if
his family secures work with one grower or agricultural firm, he
may reside in one area for a year before returning to his designated
home base. Over a few years, it is possible for a migratory child
to have experienced several of these patterns of mobility while
on the trek.

HIS LIFE ON WHEELS

When migrant families move, they travel in all types of vehicles.
Those who travel in crews are transported in buses or in open trucks

covered with tarpaulins. The buses usually are old, and have been purchased by the crew leader from school boards or transit companies. Many families travel in their own cars or trucks; some are newer models, but most are old and in need of repair. A few families own station wagons.

Traveling, for the great majority of children, means crowding into an old car or into a truck loaded with household supplies. Often, three or four members of the family will ride in the cab of the truck while others ride in the back of the open truck, on top of mattresses and other household goods, or on benches for 20 or more passengers. Boxes of personal belongings are stored under these benches, and old quilts, blankets, and pillows are used for cushions.

Whatever the way of travel, the workers never stop for the night in public lodgings. They ride all night or stop by the roadside to sleep or rest. Some families spread blankets and sleep on the ground; others sleep in their cars, trucks, or sitting up in a bus. Many migrant children travel a week or more, catching sleep as they crouch together with others in the back seat of a car or lying on the floor of a truck or bus.

Public accommodations frequently are denied, and inadequate means of meeting bodily needs and preparing food must be used. The wife of a crew leader reported, "You know, after we had filled up our eight cars and trucks at a service station, the man wouldn't let me take my sick three-year-old child to the public rest room. Some people treat us like trash. We paid for the gasoline and stopped on the side of the road after we got out of town."

Meals, while traveling, consist of food poor in quality and hastily prepared. Cheap cuts of meats, cookies, and bottled drinks are purchased from stores along the way and eaten by the side of the road.

As they travel, families do not stop to view natural scenic beauty and places of historical interest, except in an incidental way. Appreciation of nature and interest in history seldom are part of their cultural background. Moreover, the drive in search of work does not permit unnecessary stops.

The children see much of the United States while on the road, but they have little understanding of what they see. "I saw fields and fields of pretty grass when we went through Kentucky. . . . Is that where they raise those race horses?" "We crossed a lot of water on a big boat when we went to Virginia. Was that the Chesapeake Bay?" "We went through a long dark place; they said the road went under a river. Where was that?"

HOME LIFE OF THE MIGRANT CHILD

Home is an endless series of brief habitations in poorly equipped houses and makeshift accommodations. The most desirable living accommodations usually are found in the labor camps, which furnish housing units for 10 families or more. Some camps are provided by the grower on his own property for his own labor force, others are privately owned and rented for profit, while others may be owned and operated by farmer groups or organizations.

In some communities, local housing authorities operate centers which accommodate both migrant families and permanent residents from lower income brackets. Other living quarters include abandoned farmhouses scattered about in the agricultural area, or dilapidated shacks and lean-to shanties which are located just outside the corporation limits of the community, in the slum sections of the town, or behind large storage buildings or business establishments. Whatever the living quarters, they are segregated from the residential section of the community.

Living accommodations in camps vary from well-constructed cement block or wood houses of four or five rooms to one-room wooden cabins or tin shelters. In some camps, living quarters are constructed with a centrally located kitchen area and rooms on either side of a long hall. Other buildings are motel style, with one building having several rooms opening onto a porch or front entrance area. A few camps have two- and three-room apartment-type buildings, either with houses or motel-type buildings divided into apartments.

A few children live in four- or five-room houses with adequate water facilities. These homes are furnished with such conveniences as electric lights, radio, television, washing machine, and comfortable beds. These families have shrubbery and flowers growing on the lawns, and they take pride in keeping their home clean and attractive. But this type of home is the exception for migrants, and usually such a family is moving out of the migratory stream and establishing a permanent residence. Many of the larger homes in centers operated by the local housing authorities are now occupied by permanent residents who at one time were migrants.

Some children live in the apartment-type buildings. Furnishings vary according to the income and ingenuity of the parents, but generally these apartments will have beds, a cooking stove, refrigerator, tables, chairs, and other bits of furniture which make the home somewhat comfortable and livable. This type of home is usually occupied by migrants who are able to pay rent on a regular basis.

The great majority of children, however, live in one-room frame cabins or in one room of an old farmhouse.   Furnishings are meager and often consist only of cots or beds with thin mattresses, a table, a cooking stove or a two-burner oil heater, and sometimes an ice box or refrigerator. One room accommodates all the family's activities, and it is not uncommon for a family unit to have 10 to 15 members, both grandparents, a married son or daughter or both and their children, an aunt, uncle, cousin, or a friend.

Other children have less than the one-room cabin or shelter for a home. They may live in old shacks, metal lean-tos, tattered tents, backs of old trucks, abandoned packing cases, or in the grass or on the ground.

Except in the very best labor camps, homes for the most part are unsanitary. Provisions for garbage disposal are inadequate and frequently nonexistent. Screens are scarce and the shuttered windows, without glass, provide little light. Often, the only toilets available are run-down privies, the ground in back of living quarters, or utility houses, which many families use and which quickly become so filthy that disease is easily transmitted.

The shelters and cabins are unclean and unkempt. Crowded conditions make for disorderliness, and the inconvenience of carrying water from public hydrants, canals, lakes, or nearby streams adds to the task of everyday cleaning. The work schedule of the mother, as well as indifference or lethargy on the part of some parents, also contributes to the uncleanliness and untidiness.

Children's personal belongings and keepsakes are stored in a box under a bed or cot. Since there is no space for closets, clothing hangs on a nail. In many homes, shelves have been improvised from orange crates and boxes. Very few homes have a dresser with a mirror. More often a small mirror is hung above a shelf which holds a comb and some toilet articles for the entire family.

Dishes, knives and forks, and cooking utensils are at a minimum. Frequently, a child has never eaten with a fork until he enters school. Some families sit together at a table for a meal, but in many families food is given out and each child eats his portion from a bowl, pan, or plate, or carries the food in his hand.

Lack of cooking equipment, of proper refrigeration, and of time necessary for preparation of food contribute to inadequate diets. Meals consist mainly of rice, potatoes, grits, dried beans, fried foods, fried salt bacon, cheap cuts of prepared meats, cheese, and fish, with food patterns varying somewhat according to the cultural background of the parents. For example, the families from Louisiana and Mississippi will serve rice; those from South Carolina and Georgia, grits; from Tennessee and North Carolina, potatoes; and from Mexico, dried beans. Diets are lacking in the protein of milk and lean meats. Green vegetables and fresh fruits are usually available, and children eat them in raw form between meals. Since mothers do not enjoy the foods with which they work daily, they do not regularly include fruits and vegetables in the family's meals.

Children as young as six or seven years old often prepare their own meals. They fry eggs and make hot dog sandwiches, warm beans, or "fix supper" for their younger brothers and sisters when their mothers are working. Often, the children visit the camp commissary or nearby community store to buy bottled drinks, inexpensive candies, and cookies which replace regular meals.

HIS EXPERIENCES WITH MONEY

Migrant children grow up without financial security and without learning to use money wisely when they have it. Their parents have no consistent plan of spending or budgeting their money. When they are working and have money, they spend it. When they do not have it, they do without. Their sources of income are irregular. Even though some workers may earn $15 to $25 on some days during a work season, the sporadic nature of their work prevents assurance of a regular or consistent income. Irregular income, coupled with the migrants' failure to budget and to buy wisely, results in long periods when they practically are starving.

Few families can meet any kind of regular payments. Representatives of business firms often reclaim purchases—stoves, washing machines, refrigerators, radios, and sometimes television sets, as well as cars and trucks—on which a family cannot continue to pay. Some families have life insurance policies, but lose them during slack periods of work. There is evidence that many workers are being exploited by high-powered salesmen who sell commodities and insurance policies to them, emphasizing that it will cost only a few cents a week. With several bills to meet each week, although each may be under a dollar, the migrant soon has his earnings pledged, and no money remains for food and rent.

THE HEALTH PROBLEM

Some migrant children appear healthy in spite of poor housing, unsanitary conditions, inadequate diets, irregular immunizations, and frustrations caused by repeated adjustments to different situations. However, the health of the migrant child is a constant problem for both the migrant family and the local health departments.

Colds, toothaches, and earaches are common illnesses among the children. Many are small in stature and anemic-looking, and possess the symptoms of malnutrition. Many are often too sick to be in school but do not want to go home. Headaches, stomach-aches, and nausea are also frequent complaints. Children suffer from impetigo, pediculosis, and "muck sores," a disease common to mucklands when unsanitary living conditions prevail. Many have incorrect postures—stooped shoulders, projecting shoulderblades—and "chalky" bones. Few make regular visits to a dentist.

Frequently, children treat their own illnesses by old-fashioned home remedies. One boy, who had recurrent headaches, was taking from 10 to 15 aspirins daily. Upon medical diagnosis, he was found to have developed a serious kidney ailment and to be suffering from enlarged tonsils.

THE MIGRANT CHILD GROWS UP EARLY

Migrant children assume family responsibilities much earlier and to a greater extent than the average American boy or girl. Five- and six-year-olds take care of younger brothers and sisters while their mothers work. School-age boys or girls say, "Naw, I can't go to school. You see, I have to look after the little 'uns." Or, after school, "Mama's goin' to wash; I have to take care of the little 'uns." "Mama has to go to work at 3 o'clock, and I mind the kids." "I have to hurry and get the house cleaned up before they get in from work." "I have to fix supper 'cause they won't get in from work until after dark, and mama'll be too tired to cook." "I've got to iron my dress to wear to school tomorrow."

As soon as they can, children become wage earners to supplement the family income. Of many children interviewed, 90 percent volunteered information about their work experiences and reported giving all or most of the money they earned to their parents. Many said, "I don't mind working, but I wish I could keep my money." Those who did not give all their money to their parents bought their own clothes and school supplies, though a parent or an older sister usually went with them to make these purchases.

Early in life the children have a concern for money and feel responsible for helping to support their families and for making their own way. In addition to vacations, many of them work after school hours, on Saturdays, and on holidays, either in agriculture or doing odd jobs, and some skip school and work in the fields before holidays in order to buy new clothes for Easter or to have some Christmas money. They prefer the work for which they can earn the most money: "I don't like to pick cotton, but I love to pull cotton; it's easier, and I can make more money." "Sometimes I like to pick tomatoes, but some places you have to be so careful with the vines, and I can't make any time." One six-year-old girl earned enough money picking beans one summer to buy a refrigerator for her mother.

A 12-year-old Mexican girl, a member of a family of 13 children, told why she was only in the fourth grade: "I'm in the fourth, I should be in the sixth, but . . . we pick cotton and we miss lots of school. . . . In 1954, when we bought our truck, we had to pick cotton to pay, and I couldn't make my grade that year."

A 14-year-old Mexican boy explained, "We have to work, and don't go to school any place but here. . . . We meant to go to school this year but we got work, so we waited till we got here. . . . I was born in Santa Rosa [Texas] but we haven't been there in four years. . . . Last year we went to Virginia, Pennsylvania, Illinois, and New York, and then came back here."

Children related stories similar to that of a 12-year-old boy in Virginia: "I just can't come to school every day. Daddy wouldn't let me come up the road if I didn't work. . . . Last year was the first time I've gone to school here." This child had come to North-ampton County from Florida during the late spring or early summer for five consecutive years and was enrolled in school each fall during the Project. His school attendance of only 19 to 24 out of 40 to 45 days that schools were open during September and October for each year he was resident indicated his father expected him to work.

Migrant families depend on the income from their children's work: "Yes, I want my children to go to school, and I send them all I can, but you see we just have to have their help now." "Work has been awfully bad up the road this year, so when we can get work, I just have to have my children help. . . . I owe so many debts, and I gotta have enough money for rent." "My boy, he helps me in the fields every day. We just couldn't make it if he didn't."

Although there is an increasing tendency for parents to want their children to work only while on the trek, many families also want them to work at the home-base area. In Palm Beach County, many cases have been reported of families who have moved on when they learned that their children must go to school and were not permitted to work during school hours.

Work during or after school hours, in the fields or at home, hardly leaves time for recreation. What play there is usually goes unsupervised. There is little opportunity for membership in community organizations, and contact with regular residents of a community is limited to school functions. Only in the better camps are there workers who plan recreation in the form of sports, craft, and sewing clubs. Most children improvise toys from sticks, pieces of string, old automobile tires, and boxes. With few exceptions, their playgrounds, when they have time for them, are the small streams of water, mud puddles, trees, and loose dirt around their homes.

How they feel

The migrant child lives in a world few teachers know intimately. Before attempting to teach him, it is necessary to know not only his way of life, but to understand the problems created by this life and to learn how he thinks and feels about himself and others. Like all children, as he grows, he acquires a picture of the kind of person he is, of the things he can and cannot do, of the sort of person he eventually can hope to be. The picture he forms will determine greatly his success or failure in school or in life. The picture is shaped by the impact of unique forces in his life:

First, his transient way of life is a force which generally leads to insecurity. In continually pulling up roots and moving into new situations the migrant child is in constant contact with nonmigrants with whom he must cooperate and compete.

Second, his foreshortened childhood is a force which also leads to insecurity. Living in a culture which compels him to assume family responsibilities early, he experiences, by 13 or 14, what a nonmigrant child will not experience until he is 18 or older.

Third, his strong and well-defined family and ingroup relationships is a force, in contrast, which generates feelings of security. But his family insists that he take on responsibilities and become a wage earner as soon as possible—ideas that conflict with nonmigrant values. As a result, what feelings of security he has become dwarfed in significance and he feels inadequate to deal with new situations.

REJECTION BY NONMIGRANT GROUPS

Migrant children come from economically and culturally deprived groups. They do not belong to any one community. Wherever they go, they are temporary and unaccepted residents, rejected by regular members of communities and by personnel of school and social or welfare agencies who are unaware of or insensitive to the circumstances which lead to deviations from accepted patterns

23

of behavior. Early in life, they acquire the feeling of being "a nobody"; of being unwanted outside the immediate family and traveling group; of not being understood; of having other people think themselves so much better than they; of being looked down upon for the way they live.

The children, especially as they grow up and become teenagers, always comment on their feeling of being "different": "The girls look down their noses at us girls who live in the camp." "They don't invite us to their parties." "She is the best teacher I ever had because she understands me." "I want to go to school because I want to be somebody."

Not only the regular members of communities, but law enforcement officers as well generally are hostile to migrant groups. As they travel, migrants are considered special persons in the eyes of the police, and they receive special attention if they violate a law. As crews move through many areas they are followed by law enforcement officers who see that they move on and are not permitted to stop. Often, state troopers stand by and watch while the crew makes necessary stops to purchase food and gas, to have trucks and buses repaired, or to wait for a ferry in order to prevent anyone from leaving the crew.[1] There is often disorder, drinking, and fighting in the migrant camps, and the local officers are called to apprehend the offenders and to restore order.

Children come to feel singled out and punished for their migratory way of life. During the study of "community helpers" in school, many are likely to contribute first-hand information concerning policemen: "The policeman is always after you." "He goes around in his car on Saturday night to catch anyone who is drinking or fighting." He is a physical force that punishes people and puts them in jail or "reform school." When asked what the policeman did, one first-grader explained, "He puts people in jail. . . . Where we lived, they put my daddy in jail every time he went to town."

The attendance worker, known as the "truant officer," represents the same threat as the policeman. Some children make no distinction between the two public services. One boy said, "If you run away or play hooky from school the policeman will get you and take you to the reform school." Another reported, "My mama told me if we don't do our writing and work in school that she's gonna send us to the reform school." On one hand the child is threatened with punishment for nonattendance; on the other, he is kept out of school to work. Such conflicts do not help him form any consistent or favorable attitude toward school.

[1] Koos, Earl L. *They Follow the Sun.* Jacksonville: Bureau of Maternal and Child Health, Florida State Board of Health, 1957. p. 35-38.

THE SCHOOL AND ITS GOALS

As the migrant child comes in direct contact with the school, other conflicts develop in him. Discrepancies between the facts of his life and the expectations, practices, and beliefs the school holds for him become evident: "I don't know whether my folks want me to go to school or not." "My parents want me to go to work and help them, and I want to get a car." "Mother wants me to stop school, and my father wants me to go on." "I want to drop out and get me a job."

Generally, the child's behavior at school points to his short-term goals and the fact that he must live for today only. He is not likely to participate in some future school activity because his family will leave before its scheduled time: "I hope daddy stays here until school is out." "My mama has promised me that we won't move until we have our art exhibit, but I'm afraid that we will have to." "I don't know when we are moving, but just any time now, I guess."

Distant goals, therefore, are meaningless. A reward for the migrant child must be fast, certain, and tangible. The migrant girls who had finished their project in 4-H Club work were indifferent to writing up their records which would make them eligible for scholarships to the 4-H Club Camp during the summer. One explained, "I'm not going to be here anyway to go to camp this summer, so why do all that work?" However, when they discovered that they would be presented with a pin during an assembly program before they left, most of them finished their record sheets, and earned their 4-H Club pins.

At first, the migrant child is likely to be afraid of school. This fear is built up in part by his parents: "You'd better mind your teacher or she'll beat you." "I hear that principal is tough and will use his belt on you." The child hears his parents say to the teacher, "Now, just give him a good licking if he don't get his lessons." He sees the school as a policing force and develops guarded behavior which he regards as appropriate. Teachers, as a result, often find it difficult to interest the child in listening to stories, talking about his experiences, and engaging in other activities which will help him to extend his interests or deepen his understanding of the life about him. He is likely to be busy at his seat laboriously doing the only things he knows how to do, such as writing numbers or copying his ABC's or a page from a "reader book."

Feelings about school are further complicated by the attitudes of parents. Though many want their children to have an education, they accept failure for them as easily as they once accepted failure for themselves. Parents comment: "Now, he's in the fourth grade, but we've moved around, and he's behind, so you may have to put him back." "He has a hard time learnin', so he may not do very well in school."

Early in life, then, the migrant child acquires a sense of inadequacy in school. A junior high-school girl writes, "I like to go to school even though I can't learn much." A newcomer cries, "I can't do that . . . I ain't never learned much in school . . . I can't do schoolwork." Others say, "I ain't never learned to read much; you will have to put me in first grade." Or, "I ain't good at learnin'." Inevitably, irregular and short-term attendance reinforces the child's expectation of academic retardation and failure: "I'm just in the fourth grade, I should be in the sixth grade, but when we go to . . . pick cotton we don't go to school." "I don't know what grade I'm in; you see I ain't been to school much." "I know I'm behind the others, but I like it here because I'm not in the same room with the little children." A 12-year-old boy states, "I guess you'll have to put me in the second grade; I ain't never been in any school long enough to learn to read much." A 9-year-old girl cries, "I can't read a word. We've always moved around, and I ain't been to school much."

Teachers and other community workers unknowingly may add to the child's feeling of inadequacy by a thoughtless word, a gesture, or facial expression of dislike or rejection. They are often unable to understand why migrant parents will give lip service to a desire for an education for their child and yet keep him out of school at every opportunity to work in the fields, to take care of the babies, or to do the family washing and other household duties.

FRUSTRATION AND LONELINESS

Mobility creates feelings of frustration for migrant children. They feel the impact of having to make repeated adjustments to new situations. Continually, they must relate themselves to new schools, to new classmates, to new teachers, and to different methods of teaching and school organization: "About the time I make a few friends and learn about the school, we have to leave again." "I just can't catch on. It was so different in that other school where I went before I came here." "I'd like to go to school if I could go to one school all the time."

They feel the loneliness which stems from frequently moving into new areas: "I get homesick when I move away. Like now, I'm so homesick I could die. It's no fun when I have to move away." "I don't like to move because I have to make new friends and I can't make friends good." "When I move to another place I wish I had someone to play with, but I don't know anyone. After I have stayed there for a week or two I will find some pals. Then I have to move right off again and leave them." "I don't know anybody, and I feel like I'm lost."

As all children, migrants are naturally social, and they long to have friends. They speak of the friends that they have made at school, during their travels, and during work. "I like school because I have friends there, and we play together." "I like to move because I get to make some new friends sometimes." "Even in work, picking cotton is fun when you have friends working with you, and you see who can pick the most cotton."

But their friendships, of necessity, are brief. Frequently, these friendships become close within a few weeks, and the child cries when he leaves his friends: "I do not want to leave my friends. They have been so nice to me." "I always miss my friends." "I was very broken-hearted when I left him behind; I cried every night about him. . . . I walked away with tears in my eyes."

Some children express attachment for their physical surroundings when they live in one place for any length of time. In compositions they write: "I hated to leave my pet pigeons." "Mother and I had a garden planted. Then we moved and I had to leave it." "When I lived in one place I had a tree hut in my back yard that my friends and I often stayed in all night. I loved my tree hut. . . . One time I had a garden, made it all by myself, but just as it was getting pretty, we had to move away and leave it. . . . I was sad to leave our grapefruit tree in our backyard."

Some children react so negatively to traveling that they develop empathy for those who must move: "I think it's a bad thing to see someone move away with all their things on some truck. I don't like to, and I don't like to see someone else have to." "It makes me feel bad when someone has to leave. I wish that I could go instead of them."

EARLY SOCIAL MATURATION ACCENTUATES DIFFERENCES

Migrant children know little of childhood. They come from a culture in which their life pattern is geared to their biological development. From an early age their families depend on them to assume responsibilities and to work and supplement family income. As a result, they grow up faster than other children in our society.

Many of them enter into sexual relationships upon reaching biological maturity in the early teens. Early marriages are common and seem to be the accepted pattern. It is not unusual for a 14- or 15-year-old girl to quit school to marry: "This is the last time I am going to school; I am going to get married." "When you get married you don't have to go to school."

Like that of their families, the children's lives are geared to the realities of the present. The exigencies of life—the need to provide for food, shelter, and clothing—and the inability to know what tomorrow may bring make it impossible for them to plan their lives in terms of extended goals. First, immediate needs must be met; then, thought may be given to such matters as schooling. Parents say: "I have to work every day, and I just have to have Mary stay at home and help." "Yes, I intend to send them to school, but she will have to have some clothes and shoes." "It won't hurt her to miss school this week. She's missed so much already I reckon she's gonna fail anyhow."

The children's concern with family problems is evident in their preoccupations at school. A class was drawing pictures of the kinds of work their parents did. One girl who had just enrolled in school made a picture of a packing house with figures around it. A fence surrounded the packing house and outside of it stood a lone figure of a man who apparently had not found work. "This is my daddy," she pointed out.

A teacher read a story to children in a primary grade about a monkey who had no friends, no money, no home, and nothing to eat. "That's like us when we first came here," commented one of the migrant children.

One year when the crops froze, a family was put out of its shack for failure to pay the rent. The 15-year-old girl returned to school the following morning and reported to the principal, "A man gave my daddy enough money to pay the rent and they let us back in, but it ain't gonna do no good. There ain't no work and we're gonna have to leave."

Specific circumstances in their lives bring these children to early maturity. They are not protected from the hard realities of life. Even as six-year-olds, they may hear family discussions of unemployment, desertion, and adultery. They have seen much of drinking, fighting, quarreling, infidelity, encounters with the law, sickness, and death. If they have not witnessed such practices and events in their own family, they have seen them in other families.

During a talking period in school, a six-year-old child spoke: "Yesterday, I saw two men fighting. They cut each other with a knife. My daddy called the policeman." Another child adds, "I've seen lots of fights. My daddy and mama used to fight. He would get drunk. My mama would call the police, and they would put him in jail. He would fight her when he got out. He don't get drunk no more."

Fighting is seen as an event that is not unusual. It may be branded as bad behavior and the police may be called in to stop it, but it is regarded as behavior to be expected when a person is drunk, when a person needs to defend himself, or when certain codes have been violated. Parents seem to value the ability to fight and expect their children to defend themselves against attack. Early in life, the migrant child learns to protect himself.

Migrant children have much first-hand information about sickness, accidents, and death. They face these events realistically and accept them as an inevitable part of their lives. During such times they always want to do something to help—take up a collection and send food and flowers. A child reports, "My aunt's little baby died and we went down to the funeral home to see it. My mother held my little brother so he could see it too. My daddy let them have twenty-five dollars so they could take it back to Tennessee to bury it. It was all the money he had."

Although pressures are great in the lives of migrant children for them to grow up and assume responsibilities, some express hope for finishing school and bettering their lives in the future.

Some state a specific kind of job which they would like, such as becoming a teacher, nurse, or seamstress; doing construction work; driving a truck; working in a filling station or as an auto mechanic; and joining the navy.

The great majority, however, seem eager to get out of school and get a job: "I learned to drive a truck in Michigan last summer. I want to hurry and get out of school and get a job." "I'm not going to school next year if I can get out of it. I want to get a job and go to work." "My daddy said as soon as I get in high school, he's gonna get me out. He says my mama has enough work at home for me to do."

Consequently, as early as 13 years, many children are out of school and free from parental control. They may continue to live with their parents or relatives and contribute to their financial support or they may leave the family unit to be completely independent.

FAMILY COHESION AS A SOURCE OF SECURITY

Though much in the life of migrant children tends to develop insecurity, they have a source of strength in the strong relationships between themselves and their family and the reinforcing relationships with their ingroup.

Large families are common and usually family loyalties are strong. Migrant children fight in order to protect their small brother or sister. They love their family and seem to be pleased with an addition to it. They are enthusiastic over the return of an older brother or sister to live with the family or to visit.

When the family lives together as a family group, children are conscious of having both a father and mother and speak of their roles in the activities of the family. "My daddy drives Mr. Smith's truck and takes people to work, and my mama works at the packing house." "My mama and daddy are going to take us kids to the drive-in." Many, though, come from broken homes. Some insecurity is found among these children, but, on the whole, adjustment to living with a step-parent, uncle, grandmother, or with a family which is no blood relation seems to be rapid and satisfactory.

Even though relationships and patterns in the family group give the child a sense of security, they create a conflict in him when he comes in contact with the school. Decisions for the family are made autocratically by the family head. (Generally, in white and Spanish-American households, the father is head; in Negro families, the mother is head.) Children accept these decisions as final and do not question parents' judgments, but this approach conflicts with the schools' emphasis on democratic procedures. As a result, teachers have difficulty in getting the migrant child to participate in group activities. Frequently, he withdraws and offers no opinion or attempts to dominate or impose his idea on the group.

Material possessions in migrant homes are considered common belongings. Children are accustomed to sharing them freely with the other members of the family. But this pattern of behavior causes difficulty when they come to school. When a child picks up someone else's pencil and uses it as his own, he is immediately accused of taking something which does not belong to him.

Loud, boisterous, and harsh talking is common around the homes and camps. Many children hear, and sometimes use, profane language in conversations at home; but, when one of them uses such language at school, some child will say, "I'm going to tell the teacher you said a bad word" or "The teacher will punish you; you cussed" or "Did you know what you said . . . you know you can't talk that way at school." Thus, when the migrant child is behaving in a way that is natural and acceptable to him, his actions may run counter to the usually accepted patterns of behavior and practices in the school and community.

ATTITUDES REFLECT INSECURITY

Every day of their lives migrant children are aware of the differences between themselves and the nonmigrant culture—the way they live, their lack of education, their forced maturity, their overly strong family ties. They are outsiders, and they feel insecure. This feeling, evident so frequently, is one of the major problems with which the teacher must work.

The little newcomer stands at the fountain to get a drink, but seeing two other children coming toward the fountain, she steps back for them to go ahead of her. A teacher reaches out to give the new boy a friendly pat on the shoulder, and he dodges. The new boy stands aside and refuses to enter the ball game that his classmates are playing. After a week of watching he slips into a game which a group of younger and smaller boys are playing.

Teachers, in describing the specific characteristics of the children, noted their shyness, timidity, and withdrawal: "Beth is very timid and shy, and will not let her cousin move from her side." "Willie feels unwanted, and never participates voluntarily in any class discussion. . . . He is very shy of the teacher." "Carol is timid, quiet, and shy. She does not associate with other pupils, and talks only when asked a question directly." "Billy does not play with his classmates. . . . In any class or physical education activity, he makes excuses to get out of participating."

Instead of entering into group games at playtime most children stray away from organized activities. They have difficulty in learning to play with others. Since they have had little experience in organized group games, they do not understand team spirit and have not learned to accept established procedures or the rules of the game.

In order to gain attention or to avoid doing schoolwork for which he feels inadequate, a child will complain of some imaginary illness.

A 12-year-old boy could not work on the academic level of other children in his room except in arithmetic. He developed all kinds of physical ills—toothache, aching eyes, headaches, cut fingers—and constantly complained of some ache or pain during the school day. During the arithmetic period, he recovered and participated enthusiastically.

A girl complained of her eyes and repeatedly told the teacher that she could not see well enough to read. The school nurse found nothing wrong with her vision, yet the child continued to complain. The teacher and principal went to personal expense and trouble to have the child examined by an oculist. He diagnosed excellent vision with no other complications which would cause any difficulty in seeing. However, the oculist gave the child noncorrective glasses which she wore at school, and she continued to insist that she needed them to see.

Migrant children further reveal their insecurity by dependence on their teachers. Many see their teachers in a parent relationship, serving as a substitute mother or father when they feel rejected by their own.

Terry, who came from a broken home and lived with her grandmother, longed for her mother to come home and do what other mothers did for their children. She would ask, "Why don't my mama like me? Why don't she come home?" Terry became attentive and affectionate toward her teacher, and repeatedly asked to be her little girl. During the day she did not want her teacher out of her sight. Usually, she moved her chair close to her and held on to her dress.

One girl stated, "I wish . . . [the principal] was my daddy." Upon investigation, the teacher learned that the girl had an unkind stepfather, and looked upon the principal as the figure of the type of father she wanted. She thought that he was kind and good. She had seen him play with his own children, and she longed to have a father like that.

Migrant children are often belligerent toward the school and the teachers. Their insecurity manifests itself in unacceptable behavior, from making ugly remarks about a teacher to bullying smaller children and classmates. In some cases they may be guilty of more serious offenses—stealing or breaking into buildings— which must be handled by juvenile authorities.

One 11-year-old girl was rude to her teacher. After questioning by the principal, the girl explained, "Yes, I called her a bad name. The others told me that the teacher would tell the truant officer that I wasn't in school yesterday, and the truant officer will come and get me and take me to the reform school." A boy remarked, "I have had too many teachers I didn't like." A third child said, "I didn't like none of them at all. I just didn't like their ways or them."

Against the overwhelming record of insecurity among migrants, it must be noted that a few children are open to new experience and absorb learning readily. Even though they have little past experience with formal learning, they have a favorable and positive attitude toward school, their minds are still open, and they have an inner drive for accomplishment. More than likely, they can appraise their own achievements, are aware of their deficiencies, and have a clear idea of what they want to do in school. The teacher must learn to work with both groups of migrant children.

Establishing rapport

The job of working with migrant children in the schools, as seen against a background of their life and the problems it creates, requires careful preparation before teaching is even begun. How the children and their parents feel about school makes a great difference in the effectiveness of the school in meeting their needs. An analysis of written accounts submitted by teachers, as well as the experiences of the Project Supervisor, revealed that establishing rapport between teacher and child was the first important step in the process of teaching. A variety of ways was found to be successful:

1. Preparing resident children for the coming of migrant children
2. Welcoming migrant children into the schools
3. Devoting special time to migrant children
4. Encouraging the sharing of travel experiences
5. Providing for participation in special school programs and projects
6. Recognizing migrant children when they withdraw from school
7. Making friendly contacts with parents.

PREPARING RESIDENT CHILDREN

The first step, even before migrant children come into the classroom, is to prepare resident children for their arrival. Teachers made use of a wide range of classroom activities to insure the acceptance of the migrants when they came. They held class discussions on the importance of being friendly and kind to the newcomers and making them feel at home. They explained that many of the children spoke Spanish and, as a result, that the permanent members of the class would be fortunate to have the opportunity of learning Spanish expressions. Finally, teachers described the lives of migrants, their travels and their work with crops, and read books and showed films about them.[1]

One teacher, for example, read *Judy's Journey* [2] to her class. Together, they discussed the book and how Judy must have reacted to the different treatment which she received from the children at school. In turn, Judy's experiences were related to those of the children who would be coming to their classroom, and they discussed what they should do to make them feel welcome in their classroom, and what they should not do. The children were ready to accept the new pupils as they came in during the year. "There were no ugly attitudes toward them," the teacher reported, "and the migrant children seemed happy and well-adjusted, and with the help of the other children began to participate freely in activities."

WELCOMING MIGRANT CHILDREN

Many methods were devised for welcoming the migrant child into the school: introducing the child to the group, assigning the child a "big brother" or "big sister," recognizing his coming in the morning "news story," assigning him a special duty or membership on a classroom committee, and recognizing his enrollment through displays on the bulletin boards and a story in the school newspaper.

The Migrant Child Is Introduced

Introductions were made by the teacher or by a pupil who had been assigned the responsibility. Facts about the newcomer were reported, such as the school he had attended, the state from which he had moved, and the activities in which he was interested. In the event the newcomer was Spanish-speaking, the teacher would mention that he knew two languages or that he spoke Spanish and "we are going to help him to learn to speak English." Whenever possible, if the child was unable to speak English, interpreters helped with the introductions.

---

[1] The following have been identified:

A *Desk for Billie*. (Film) 57 min., 16mm, sound, color and b & w. National Education Association, Division of Press and Radio Relations, 1201 Sixteenth Street, N.W., Washington 6, D. C., 1956.

Gates, Doris. *Blue Willow*. New York: Viking, 1940. 172 p.

Lenski, Lois. *The Strawberry Girl*. Philadelphia, Penn.: Lippincott, 1945. 193 p.

— *Cotton in My Sock*. Philadelphia, Penn.: Lippincott, 1949. 190 p.

— *Judy's Journey*. Philadelphia, Penn.: Lippincott, 1947. 212 p.

McGehee, Florence. *Please Excuse Johnny*. New York: Macmillan, 1952.

Williams, Vinnie. *The Fruit Tramp*. New York: Harpers, 1957. 247 p.

[2] Lenski, Lois, *op. cit.*

A Buddy Helps Him

A "big brother" or "big sister" helped the newcomer become oriented to his surroundings and acquainted with the other children. He also was responsible for taking the newcomer on a tour of the school; accompanying him to the bathroom, lunchroom, library, and playground; explaining to him about the classroom activities and the general routine of organization; arranging for him to have paper, pencils, and books during the first few days; and serving as a special friend to help him feel that he was welcome in the school. Frequently, teachers reported that the migrant child would volunteer to be "buddy" for the next newcomer.

His Name Appears in the Morning "News Stories"

The morning "news stories" were used to welcome the migrant children, especially in the primary grades. The stories were developed out of a morning "sharing" period:

Our News	Hello, Margaret
Today is Monday.	We have a new girl.
We have a new pupil.	Her name is Margaret.
Her name is Betty Jean.	She rides three days to get to Belle Glade.
She is from Fort Pierce, Florida.	Her father hauls apples in Michigan.
Welcome! Betty Jean.	Welcome! Margaret.

Our New Friends
We have three new children in our room today. Their names are Annie Mae, Ruby, and James. Ruby and Annie Mae came from Springfield, New York, and James has been in Milton, Delaware. Later they will move to Florida. We are glad to have them with us. We want them to like our school, and we hope they will come back next year.

Special Classroom Responsibilities Are Given Him

After this introductory orientation, teachers helped the child feel a member of the group by assigning him to a special job and having him share in room responsibilities and take his turn as a member of classroom committees. These experiences included distributing and collecting supplies, watering plants, and making trips to the office, and more responsible jobs such as leading games and serving as team captain or as chairman of classroom projects.

Mary, an 8-year-old migrant girl, was shy, timid, and withdrawn. Her teacher wrote, "I wanted her to take part in every activity around her and to enjoy associating with the other children. . . . I gave her the things to do which would cause her to mingle with the other children." These jobs included passing out books, papers, and supplies, and sharpening pencils for her group; taking reports to the office; and serving as leader when the children went to and from the bathroom and playground. At times, during play periods the teacher arranged for her to be chosen as game leader. "I noticed that she seemed to get a feeling of belonging and learned to play with the other children. . . . They chose her as their partner in games and chose to sit with her sometimes in the classroom," the teacher reported. She left after four weeks, but "she seemed happy to be with us, and hated to leave."

Bulletin Board Displays Announce His Enrollment

Many teachers adopted the practice of writing the names of new-comers on the blackboard. Other teachers arranged displays on classroom bulletin boards or special charts which were hung in the room. Such captions as "These Are Our New Friends" and "Welcome Newcomers" were used. A few schools arranged for the names of all new students to be placed on bulletin boards in the corridors.

In one school, Hosea, a boy who had entered during mid-season the previous year, but had enrolled upon the opening date of the current year, checked the bulletin board. Not finding his name, he went into the principal's office and exclaimed to the principal, "You forgot to put my name on the bulletin board." She explained to him that those names represented all the children who had entered since school began, and since he had been a student the year before he was not a newcomer. Sensing his disappointment she added, "Hosea, we consider you one of us now, and we need you to help us welcome all our newcomers this year." Satisfied by the explanation, he smiled, but as he hurried out the door, he added, "My name will oe up there next year for we're going up the road next summer."

School Papers Feature Arrivals

Attention was called in school papers to the entrance of migrant children.

One bimonthly school paper published by a sixth-grade class contained a column, "Goings-On in the Grades." A special feature of the column was an introduction to the new children by members of the newspaper staff. These articles recorded the travels, hobbies, and interests of each child. The purpose of this project, according to the teacher in charge, was "to make the readjustments of migrant children a bit easier by giving them some of the notoriety all children enjoy and by attempting to instill in other students interest in them as individuals."

Most teachers believed that these practices of welcoming migrant children into the school helped to establish rapport:

"Terry associates with the other pupils and contributes to class discussions. She has overcome some of her shyness and has less tendency toward being an introvert."

"Children became better adjusted; they learned to work well with the group and seemed to feel that they were needed in the classroom."

"All the children liked Johnny, and he was 'one of the boys' at school. The class has bought his big picture which came after he left, and are saving it for him when he returns next spring or fall."

Not all attempts at orientating the migrants were successful. Reports revealed that some children left school without having adjusted. However, in almost all of these accounts the teachers stated that the children did not stay long enough, having been enrolled in school for no more than three weeks.

DEVOTING SPECIAL TIME TO MIGRANT CHILDREN

Teachers provided extra time for contacts with the migrant children and they used it for talking with them and giving them individual help to make them comfortable and at ease, overcome their timidity, and feel that they belonged to the group. Some teachers used the extra time for guidance and counseling in behavior acceptable for school and society; personal cleanliness, hygiene, and grooming; the importance of coming to school; jobs for which the pupil might prepare; spending and saving money earned; and the importance of going to Sunday school and church. Other teachers helped the child individually with his schoolwork, giving him extra drills and materials for independent work and magazines and books to read.

For the most part individual help took place during the school day—in the classroom, on the playground, and during a free period or lunch hour. However, there were some accounts of teachers having talked with a child on the way home, on the street, in stores, or while visiting his home.

A 16-year-old high-school boy in one school did not attend classes regularly and made poor grades in all subjects. From personal interviews with the boy, the teacher felt that if he were given an opportunity to excel in something, he would do better work generally. She talked with him about his work and learned that he could not drive a truck. She pointed out to him the additional opportunities he might have in the harvesting of crops if he had a

driver's license, and encouraged him to enroll in the driver education course. He joined the class and became one of the top pupils.
He came to school regularly and was a much better adjusted pupil.
Teachers reported that his work had improved, and that "he was
a different person."

A 10-year-old Spanish-speaking boy, who had no vocabulary in
English, was placed in a third-grade classroom. His teacher arranged for extra periods to work with him individually. By using
objects and pictures, she made the boy understand that she wanted
him to say each word in Spanish for her so that she could learn
it. She watched the child's mouth as he pronounced the word in
Spanish, then in English. In turn, the child watched the teacher's
mouth as she pronounced the English word, after which he said the
word in English. Both acted as teachers and both as learners. In
this way, rapport was established between child and teacher, and
he made rapid progress in speaking English.

Seven migrant children, one whose native language was Spanish,
enrolled in a seventh-grade arithmetic class two months after
school had begun. The teacher held interviews with these pupils
during her free period and after school hours. Since she spoke
Spanish, she was able to converse with the Spanish-speaking girl
and gain insight into her personal needs. These conversations
in Spanish pleased the girl very much and delighted the other
children who picked up a few Spanish expressions. The teacher
was able to identify special needs of these children not only in
arithmetic but in English and give them additional help so they
could participate in the regular classroom work with the other
children. "Now," she stated, "these newcomers are well-liked and
accepted by the others. They are learning rapidly and want to continue in school here."

Throughout their written accounts, teachers mentioned the need
for more time to spend individually with migrant children. The
more time, the better the opportunity for the teacher to become
acquainted with each child as a person and to know his background,
his interests, his experiences, his aspirations, and his feelings, and
for the migrant child to learn that his teacher is a friend who wants
to help him. Teachers report:

"This interest, love, affection, and additional attention . . . gave
the child security and a sense of belonging. Within two weeks she
reacted as a normal child would, and became an average pupil in
her grade."

"Kenneth realized the responsibility he had accepted. He became
interested in school and is an average student. The part-time job
in the hardware store helps, and he is making an excellent em-

ployee. I keep in close contact with both his schoolwork and his job."

"Billy is very happy . . . plays with the boys. I think he feels that we want him and that we are his friends."

"He is attending school every day . . . does good work, and he told me the other day that he never thinks of stealing anything now."

ENCOURAGING THE SHARING OF
TRAVEL EXPERIENCES

One of the best opportunities to help migrant children feel important, as well as accepted by their peers, was to have them tell of their travel experiences. All teachers in some way provided this opportunity by having the children name the states in which they had traveled, the kinds of work they had done, the scenes they had viewed, the communities in which they had lived, and the schools they had attended.

One teacher wanted to help a group of children "feel at home and realize that they had interesting and valuable contributions to make." During the morning sharing period she asked each child to name the state in which he was born and the states in which he had traveled. Each child told of his experiences in these states, such as picking cotton in Missouri and Arkansas and gathering fruit in Michigan. The next day the others brought pictures of what they had seen, including post cards and clippings from magazines of mountains, lakes, and bridges. Many of the pictures collected by resident children were identified by the migrant children. This activity led into a study of agricultural crops in the different states in which the migrant children had lived. The experience created a friendly attitude among all the pupils and was the major factor in improved attendance. The migrants had a feeling that it was their school, and interest and enthusiasm in schoolwork increased.

An outline map of the United States was given to James, who, with the help of the teacher, identified the eight Southeastern states in which he had traveled. The map was placed on the bulletin board, and during the sharing period he was asked to tell about the different fruits and vegetables which grew in these states. Other children became interested and asked questions. James told how people in southern Florida climb palm trees and shake down coconuts; how members of his crew had gathered grapes, apples, and peaches; and how they had picked strawberries, beans, and tomatoes and gathered potatoes in Delaware and Virginia. The teacher reported that from this experience he gained approval of the group and developed a sense of security and of being wanted.

By providing opportunities for migrant children to share their travel experiences, teachers found that rapport was established and that possibilities were developed for the use of these experiences in teaching the child:

"Pupils became happy members of the group. They have learned to express themselves more freely and interestingly, and all of us have learned more about life in other communities and states."

"Charles gained a feeling of belonging, a sense of security and status with his peers. During social studies the next day he was one of the first five children chosen by the group to give special oral reports."

"This group activity helped the migrant children to overcome their timidity and shyness, and to adjust socially. They were well-liked by their classmates, and were interested in coming to school every day."

PROVIDING FOR PARTICIPATION IN SPECIAL PROGRAMS AND PROJECTS

Migrant children participated in a variety of special school programs and classroom projects adapted to their special interests and specific needs. At the same time, the resident children became more aware of the contributions which some of the migrant children could make, and came to accept them more readily. Activities included participation in the regular classroom and all-school programs, such as general assemblies, holiday programs, dramatics, art exhibits, and band and choral concerts; participation in special school activities, such as May Day festivals, holiday floats and parades, picnics and trips, Junior Red Cross, and 4-H Clubs; and participation in teaching resident children crocheting, words and phrases in Spanish, dances, folk songs, ballads, and stories.

A migrant child transferred to one school, from a school in Mexico, soon after the Christmas holidays. He could not speak any English. During music class the teacher observed that he enjoyed music and was very rhythmical. Since she had some knowledge of Spanish she was able to tell him that the children would like to learn a Spanish dance, and that he was the person to teach one to them. He was delighted and chose the calypso. He first taught the dance to his teacher and the music teacher who helped to interpret his directions to the children. All the children were enthusiastic about learning the dance. Musical instruments and Spanish costumes were obtained, and the dance was featured during the May Day program. The Mexican child was accepted by the class, and he learned to speak English rapidly.

Final rehearsals for an annual Christmas pageant were in progress. Marvin, a newcomer, was a polio victim who wore leg braces and walked with a noticeable limp. One day the principal discovered him crying in the corridor and realized that he required special attention to give him a "sense of being wanted and needed in the school." He arranged for Marvin to appear in the pageant as one of the three shepherds and for the shepherds' costumes to be redesigned to cover the children's legs. The principal commented, "The sincerity—and the limp—with which Marvin played his role gave the scene a human touch it had never before achieved. This experience effected a complete change in Marvin's general attitude. He developed seemingly overnight a new personality—much for the better. Interest in schoolwork increased. When he had to move a few weeks later, he wept . . . again, but for a completely different reason."

A visit to the high school was planned for a group of sixth-grade children, more than half of whom were migrants. The principals believed that this experience would help encourage them to continue school and prepare them for entrance into high school. The date was set for early spring, before the children began to withdraw from school. Prior to the visit, the teacher discussed with the group acceptable behavior when they visited the classes, the cafeteria, and the library; the kinds of questions they might like to ask; and other details which would give them confidence during the visit.

On arriving at the school, the children were greeted by members of the student council who escorted them to the principal's office where they were introduced to the principal, the class sponsors, and the office personnel. They toured the building, visited the seventh-grade classrooms, and talked with the teachers, who discussed with them the different courses offered and the various school activities in which they could participate.

After the visit the children were less reluctant about changing schools. They gained more self-assurance and some feelings of belonging to the high school. Many of them expressed a desire to finish high school.

RECOGNIZING MIGRANT CHILDREN WHEN THEY WITHDRAW FROM SCHOOL

Recognition of migrant children when they withdraw from school is important. Teachers often mentioned to the group that certain children were leaving, that they were going to miss them, and that they hoped the children would come back again next year. Resident children talked with the migrant child about his leaving, showed interest in his travels, and told him good-bye. Teachers and classmates wrote letters to the departing children, going-away parties were held and gifts and souvenirs were presented, and the names of the children who were leaving were placed on bulletin boards, written in morning news stories, and mentioned during assembly programs.

During the morning talking period in one school a first-grade teacher explained to the children that Bill would be leaving that day. She said to him, "It has been so nice that you have been with us these past weeks. I have enjoyed having you here as one of my little boys in this room, and I do hope you can come back next year." Then she said to the children, "I am going to miss Bill, aren't you?" The children's responses made Bill feel that they liked him and were really going to miss him. He said, "I like school here, too," and smiled. A few mornings later, Jim, another migrant boy, stated during the talking period, "I am going to leave, and you are going to miss me, too, like you miss Bill."

Halloween was approaching, and a seventh-grade class planned a party. Two of the migrant boys, it was learned, were leaving before the celebration. The children agreed to have the party two days earlier and chose the boys to lead the Halloween parade in honor of their departure. The next year these boys returned to the school and the teacher reported, "They act just like the other children; I can't tell the difference this year."

A teacher learned that Ulysses, a seventh-grade migrant boy, was returning to Belle Glade within a few days. The pupils and teacher planned that each of them would write to him. In turn, Ulysses wrote a letter which was placed in the class scrapbook. His mother was delighted: "Ulysses got the nicest letter from his teacher today . . . . That's the nicest thing that has ever happened to my boy . . . and every one of his classmates wrote him a letter, too. "I'm always going to keep that letter," she said. "We sure do like that teacher and that school."

A first-grade teacher, through a group experience with her class, composed a letter for one boy to take with him: "Dear Jimmie: We will miss you very much. We hope you will come back. Your Friends." When given the letter, Jimmie carefully folded it, placed it in the top pocket of his overalls, and smiled.

Results of Receiving Recognition Persist

Teachers believe that recognition given to migrant children when they leave school has favorable results. The children like school better and will enter school more promptly when they return to the area. And when they do return, they adjust more readily. Recognition, too, makes them feel important, helps to create a desire on the part of parents to enroll their children in school in other localities, and encourages them to notify teachers when they plan to leave, thereby facilitating the transfer of school records. Teachers report:

"Jack says that he is going to go to school this year when they move."

"These children come back for a few weeks every year, and they always seem glad to be here."

"Mary comes by to see me often, although it has been three years since I taught her."

"Upon Bill's return the next year, he readily became a member of the group."

MAKING FRIENDLY CONTACTS WITH PARENTS

Contacts with parents are important for increasing enrollment in school and for helping the child, as well as the parents, adjust to school once he is there. For the most part contacts were made by visits to the homes of parents and to the camps where they lived and by letters of welcome and informal notes sent to the parents with the children.

In Virginia, meetings between parents and school personnel were arranged with the assistance of a minister and camp managers. They were scheduled as families moved into the area to encourage attendance of children in school, and were successful in increasing enrollment.

Generally, home visits were made to enroll children in school, to determine causes for absences from school, and to become acquainted with the parents—to learn of the home conditions and to establish rapport with the family.

On home visits, school personnel often found that health and economic conditions necessitated immediate welfare assistance. Contacts were made with health departments, agencies, and church and charitable groups, so that food, clothing, and medical services could be furnished to families. Attendance workers also arranged for additional clothing for children so they could enroll in school.

Repeated visits were necessary in order to establish desired rapport with families. Teachers found a sincere, friendly, and informal introduction to the family; a natural conversational approach; a sympathetic, understanding, and helpful attitude toward their problems; and an invitation to visit the school and contact the teacher whenever necessary to be good methods in approaching parents.

Home Visits Help

An attendance worker visited a family who had recently moved into the community. "Their living standards were deplorable," he wrote, "and they had little food and clothing. He spent much time talking with the father and listening to his misfortunes. He learned that the man's six children had always been required to work and had attended school very little. He sympathized with the man about his problems and assured him that things would be different now that he and his wife had secured work and his children could go to school. He explained to him that his children could learn to read and write if they had the chance to go to school. He offered his assistance which the man accepted gratefully and left with the promise to return the next day. He collected clothing and shoes for the children, checked with the man's employer and explained the necessity of his having regular work, arranged with a local grocery store for credit to be extended until the man could receive pay for his work, and arranged for the school to furnish free lunches to the children until the parents could pay at least some of the cost. He continued to visit the family regularly. They were most appreciative and always welcomed him. The children enrolled in school and attended regularly during the year and a half the family lived in the area.

Arrangements were made through Maria and Lupe by two teachers—one of whom had some knowledge of the Spanish language—to visit their mother, who spoke no English, one afternoon after school. They were received warmly and graciously. Greetings were exchanged in Spanish, and conversation began with questions to an older sister who had just returned from Mexico. The teachers asked Maria's mother for help in filling out some school forms. One teacher and Maria interpreted the questions in Spanish, the older sister wrote the information in Spanish, and the other teacher checked on the accuracy of the translation.

After the school forms were completed, the teachers asked to be helped with their Spanish pronunciation, and Maria, her mother, and sister pronounced words for the teachers to repeat. Both the mother and sister expressed a desire to learn English, but their work schedules prevented getting together.

The mother inquired of the children's progress in school, and was told it was nice to have them, and that Maria was specially helpful in interpreting Spanish for the teachers.

Time passed rapidly and realizing that the mother must go to work, the teachers got up to leave. They thanked Maria's family for their hospitality and for their help with the school records and with Spanish. The mother and daughter told them that they were glad to have them visit and asked them to come again.

After the visit, relationships at school between Maria and Lupe and the teachers improved, and they seemed happier and frequently referred to "the time my teacher went home with me." The following week while the teachers were on their way to visit a family living nearby, Maria and Lupe's mother came out and greeted the teachers, and Maria went with them to identify the right house. Later, the mother came to school to ask one teacher for help in filling out some legal papers.

The results of all visits to migrant homes, however, were not as successful as the one to Maria's family. Unsuccessful experiences were reported by principals and attendance workers. Many families seemed determined that their children work.

One parent said, "I came down here in order for my 10 children to work, and I don't intend to send them to school while we're here." The next day, upon a return visit, the attendance worker found that the family had moved.

Other reports noted that parents did not seem to appreciate the assistance given—clothing, food, free rent—but the children attended school regularly and seemed happy while the parents lived in the area. One teen-age boy, whose family had received much assistance the previous year, enrolled in school promptly upon their return to the area. He told the principal, "I owe these good people here my enrolling in school."

Teachers Send Letters of Welcome

Along with personal meetings, letters of welcome and informal notes were helpful in establishing rapport with parents.

More direct results were achieved from the letters of welcome used in Virginia than in Florida. For the most part, letters increased the interest of migrant parents in sending their children to school regularly and in receiving school transfer records. Since parents rarely send children to school while on the trek, this kind of written recognition was most unusual. Yet almost all the letters requesting that a portion be filled out and returned to the school were sent back, even though much of the information was incomplete.

Parents made favorable comments about the letter:

"I had the nicest letter from the teacher today, and I'm sure going to visit the school before we leave."

"That's the first time I've ever had a teacher write me and tell me that she was glad to have one of my kids in school."

"I'll sure let you know when we're leaving so that every child in my crew will get his report card."

The minister and the camp managers, each of whom had received a copy of the letter, reported that several of the parents had brought the letters for them to read.

One manager said, "Of course, I read the letters as though I don't know anything about them. . . . I tell each of them that it surely is a nice letter and that I know now that they will want to keep their children in school every day, and all of them say that they are going to try."

The minister, who knew each parent and was always in contact with them and the children, commented, "You know, these letters which the teachers give to these children mean so much to these people. . . . Many of the parents have said so to me."

The wife of a crewleader, accompanied by 12 children, came to the school one day and explained, "We are leaving tomorrow. I've been here before, but I told all of our crew that these teachers had written to us and asked us to let them know when we were leaving, and that we must not leave without telling them." The woman visited every classroom with the child from that room, and saw that each one was properly withdrawn from school, and that he said good-bye to his teacher and classmates. Before coming, she had contacted the principal and explained that these children traveled in her crew and that they were leaving the next day. After expressing appreciation for what the school had done for the children, she had told the principal good-bye and said she would be back next year. She also had asked his permission to visit each of the classrooms. This migrant mother, throughout the three years of the Project, was a loyal supporter of the school, encouraged the children to attend regularly, and served unofficially as liaison to the Project Supervisor in identifying newcomers to the area. Through her the Supervisor learned of other migrant children who lived on private farms off the regular school bus route and was able to arrange with the superintendent for extension of the bus route in order to accommodate these children.

Another migrant mother appeared at a PTA meeting and said, "I got your letter, and I wanted to come." She was welcomed by the group and seemed to enjoy the meeting. She lived in the community only three weeks, but during that time she contributed to the cafeteria drive which the association was sponsoring, bought paint for the school to be used for eliminating a glaring light through some upper windows, and paid all of the book fees and other incidental school costs for her child. She returned to the school and expressed to the teacher and principal her appreciation for what they had done for her child, and said that she was very pleased with her daughter's progress in school.

Though these two cases were unusual, they do indicate changes in attitude that can take place when migrant parents are made to feel that they are welcome in the school and community.

Informal Notes Serve a Variety of Purposes

Informal notes were often sent to migrant families. They were used to inform them of school activities and programs, to announce services offered by the health department, to obtain additional information for school records, and to recognize and praise the migrant child for some school activity which he had done well. The teachers also wrote very brief notes or made favorable comments on the margins of written papers which the children took home to the parents:

"I wanted you to see this nice drawing Tom did today."

"We are glad that Mary is learning to write so well. I thought that you would be interested in seeing this nice paper."

"Look what your boy did today. He did not miss one of his arithmetic problems."

"Will you please listen to Flora while she tells you the interesting story she read today?"

A teacher, who had learned that a migrant family would move from the area before the arrival of the school pictures, wrote a note to the mother. She mentioned the cost of the school pictures, but explained that she was under no obligation to buy them. If the mother did wish to take the pictures, the teacher would be glad to mail them to her if she would send her the mailing address. The mother sent the money for the pictures and included a request that the teacher keep the pictures until she knew her address. Later, the teacher received a card from the mother, who was in Missouri, and mailed the pictures to her. The mother in turn acknowledged the receipt of the pictures.

Efforts To Establish Rapport Prove Valuable

Teachers agree such activities as letter-writing helped to establish rapport between the migrant children and residents and between migrant families and teachers. When such rapport was established during one school enrollment, the child felt more at home and adjusted more readily when he returned to that school. Teachers write:

"Mary comes by to talk with me frequently even though it has been three years since I taught her."

"Upon his return in November, John rushed up to his teacher and exclaimed, 'I'm back!' He found three or four of his buddies from the past school year and went right to work on the project in which the group was engaged."

"Sue is grown now and married, but after eight years I still hear from her. She has never forgotten those five months she was in school here."

Migrant parents were encouraged to visit the school and contact the teachers. Even though these visits are not generally made by the great majority of parents, an increasing number did come. One teacher reported, "Donnie's mother came to see me and talked with me about her progress in school. She thanked me for what I had done to help Donnie."

Sylvia, who had been in school six weeks during the fall months, returned to the area one week before the end of the term. Her mother called to ask if her daughter could go to school the following week. On the first day she went to school, Sylvia carried a gift-wrapped box. She had a gift for her teacher. "I don't remember her name," she said, "but I will know her when I see her." The teacher greeted her, called her by name, thanked her for the gift, and, in turn, the children welcomed her. Several children shifted chairs so that Sylvia could sit with them. Later, the mother said, "Sylvia has been so happy at school this week. She came home excited because the children and teacher had remembered her name and they were so glad to see her." The mother added that her daughter was reading every night and working on her number combinations. "We sure do like that school, and Sylvia does well here," she said.

Knowing the child academically

An even more difficult problem than that of establishing rapport with migrant children entering school is the problem of placing them in classes to best meet their needs. Since the great majority are retarded academically, and since they attend school irregularly, an accurate, rapid placement of each child, so that he may derive the most good from the time he spends in school, is essential. This placement for best learning involves two major decisions: determining the classroom or grade in which the child is to be placed and determining his attainment levels and special interests and abilities so that learning experiences may be provided to meet his specific needs.

In the process of evaluation, first consideration was given to the age, physical maturity, and social development of each child, and he was placed in a classroom accordingly. Records may have designated enrollment in a primary grade, but usually the procedure was to place a child in a more advanced grade and adapt the curriculum by taking into account his individual levels of attainment.

After a child had been placed in a classroom, three methods were found useful in determining the child's attainment levels in the skill subjects, the significant gaps in his learning, and his special interests and abilities: individual conferences and informal observations of him, specially prepared diagnostic sheets and informal classroom tests, and study of school records and reports.

INDIVIDUAL CONFERENCES AND OBSERVATIONS

Observations and individual conferences were useful in giving teachers some understanding of the instructional needs, special interests, and abilities of the children.

A teacher learned much by observing a child as he began to explore and use materials in the classroom, as he selected books from the reading shelf, and as he talked about his experiences.

The "planned interview" conference revealed information informally. Interest inventories and lists of questions were developed and used as guides during these initial conferences. Sometimes older children were asked to write answers to a prepared list of questions, including:

Where did you live before you came here? Were you in school? What did you like to do best in that school? Why?

In what states have you lived? Can you name some crops that grow in these states? What crops do you like to work in best?

How many brothers do you have? Does your mother work away from home? Do you have suppers at home with your family? Do you stay at home with your family during the evenings? Do you like to do this?

Do you have a hobby? Do you like to travel? Are the boys and girls in other states nice to you? Do you have friends? Do you ever write to them? [1]

Observations made during visits to the homes and camps also were helpful. Through these observations and the casual and planned interviews teachers became familiar with children and were able to identify some of their instructional needs.

SPECIALLY PREPARED DIAGNOSTIC SHEETS AND EXERCISES

Series of diagnostic exercises were prepared and used. (See p. 55-65.) Geared to different instructional levels of reading, arithmetic, spelling, and language, they were designed to draw on the kinds of unique travel and work experiences with which the migrant child is familiar. They were used primarily to identify instructional needs and to ascertain attainment levels. However, teachers reported that they also provided interesting and meaningful activities for the child the first days in school.

In the use of these exercises, care was taken so that the child would not feel he was being tested and so that he would feel able to succeeed in his schoolwork. Teachers recommended that an adequate supply of these exercises, representing several levels of [2]

---

[1] This list is adapted from several lists developed by teachers during the Project: *A Guide to the Education of Agricultural Migratory Children, op. cit.,* p. 61-62; *Working with Migrant Children in Our Schools, op. cit.,* p. 33-35; *A Guide to the Teaching of Reading,* p. 23-24.

[2] Text continued on p. 66.

DIAGNOSTIC EXERCISES

Pre-Primer Level

Name

Come, mother.

Come and see.

Come and see my beans.

Draw a line from each of these words to the picture.

(To be read by teacher)

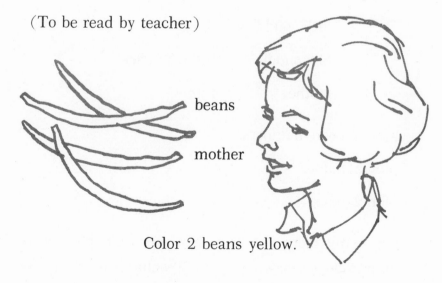

beans

mother

Color 2 beans yellow.

Color 1 bean green.

Primer Level

Name _____

> One day it rained.
> Down came the rain.
> The rain made little puddles.
> The rain made big puddles.
> Mother could not pick beans.

Draw a line from the word or phrase in the first column
to the matching word or phrase in the second column.
(To be read by teacher)

rain	mother
down	big puddles
little puddles	down
big puddles	little puddles
mother	rain

Draw 7 bean hampers.

Color 5 red.

Color 2 blue.

How many more red bean hampers than blue bean
hampers do you have?_____ (Teacher reads the question and tells child "bean hampers")

First-Grade Level

Name: _____ Day: _____

> John works on a big farm.
> On the farm are many beans.
> There are many potatoes, too.
> John helps to pick the beans.
> He likes to work in beans.
> He helps to pick up the potatoes.
> He does not like to work in potatoes.
> Big trucks come to the farm.
> John rides in the big trucks.
> He likes to ride in the big trucks.

Write "Yes" or "No" to each of these questions. (To be read by teacher)

> The farm is a little farm. _____
>
> John likes to pick the beans. _____
>
> He likes to pick up potatoes. _____
>
> The trucks are red. _____
>
> John likes to ride in the trucks. _____
>
> Draw 6 trucks.
>
> How many trucks do you have? _____

Draw 4 more trucks. Color 4 trucks red.

How many trucks are left? $6+4=$ _____ $10-6=$ _____

Color these trucks green. $4+6=$ _____ $10-4=$ _____

How many green trucks left? _____

Second-Grade Level

Name: _____ Date: _____

Fisherman Pete

Early one morning we went fishing. Mama, Daddy, Jim, and I went to the dike. We fished for a long, long time, but the fish did not bite. By and by the sky became cloudy; then it began to rain. But we did not leave because we wanted to catch some fish. After awhile the fish began to bite. Mama caught five fish and daddy caught only two. Jim caught four, but I caught seven. Then they called me "Fisherman Pete."

Add *ed* to these words: call   fish   rain

Make a sentence that asks a question with one of your new words.

How many fish did they catch together? _____

How many more fish did Mama catch than daddy? _____

How many more fish did Jim catch than daddy? _____

How many fish did "Fisherman Pete" and Jim catch together? _____

On the back of your paper you may draw the fishing party. Color it as you like.

Third-Grade Level

The Fair Comes to Town

John was up early this morning. There were three days of the year when John never slept late—Christmas, his birthday, and the day the fair came to town. He dressed hurriedly and rushed downstairs. "Is breakfast ready, Mother?" he asked.

Today was not John's birthday. It was not Christmas either. Oh my, no! It was the day that John liked best, and it was going to be a lovely fall day. Outside the window John could see the twittering birds flitting from branch to branch in the old oak tree, and he could hear the wind rustling the brightly colored leaves.

Why did John hurry to breakfast? ....

....

The day John liked best was ....

Christmas comes in the month of..

Choose five picture words from the story. ....

....

There are 31 days in December and there are 30 days in June, but there are only 28 days in February. How many days are there in the three months?..............

How many more days has December than February?

Can you solve these problems?

```
  8    9    4    3
 x3   x2   x5   x6   2) 18    3) 24    4) 20    3) 18
```

Fourth-Grade Level

Peanut Man

Someday you may go to the Everglades of Florida and live on Lake Okeechobee. If you do you will want to meet "Peanut Man." His real name is Sheelly Pouncy, but everybody calls him "Peanut Man" because he sells peanuts. He is a very industrious person who is well-liked by all citizens, especially the children.

He peddles his peanuts on the streets. Some of the peanuts are parched and some are boiled. Children rush from all directions to buy a bag of peanuts which he sells for 10¢. While munching on the fresh peanuts they learn that his wife parches, boils, and bags the peanuts at their home.

How Well Have I Read?

1. This story tells about _____
2. Why is "Peanut Man" liked by citizens? _____
3. Find one word in the story that means to eat. _____
4. Lake Okeechobee is located in _____
5. Peanut Man is liked best by: citizens_____ adults_____
   children_____ (Check the correct word)

Can You Work These Problems?

1. Peanut Man sells 50 bags of peanuts. How much money does he get?

2. If the peanut man sells 122 bags of peanuts on Monday, 300 bags on Tuesday, and 125 on Wednesday, how many bags does he sell in three days?_____

3. If he sells 56 bags of peanuts in the morning and 47 in the afternoon, how many bags does he sell that day?_____

4. He sold 73 bags of parched peanuts and 45 bags of boiled peanuts. How many more bags of parched peanuts did he sell than boiled?_____

Fifth-Grade Level

Read this story carefully. Then answer each question below the story by filling in the blanks with the right words.

Christmas Surprise

Bill and Betty, Father and Mother arrived at the ranch late on Christmas Eve. Almost before Father had stopped the car, the children were racing toward the house where Grandma and Grandpa Banks were waiting for them. A hot supper was waiting, too. Even the beds seemed waiting for Bill and Betty to climb into them as soon as supper was finished. Grandma Banks insisted that everyone go to bed early. "No late sleeping on Christmas morning," she said.

Before daylight a tinkle of bells floated through the house. Bill and Betty tumbled out of bed and raced down to the big front room. There was Grandpa standing with a big package in his hands and a smile on his face. There were gifts for everyone under the tree. At breakfast everyone seemed happy, but Grandpa seemed to be the happiest of all.

His eyes twinkled when Grandma said, "The best gift is in the barn. Get dressed and let's go out." A secret! The children could see it shining in Grandma's eyes. Everyone rushed out to see what was in the barn. What boy or girl ever had a bigger or better surprise? There stood a beautiful brown pony. The children were so excited. They knew that they were the happiest children in the whole wide world.

While visiting Grandma, Bill and Betty gathered eggs for her. Grandma gave them 10¢ for each dozen eggs they gathered. The first day they found 4 dozen eggs; the second day they gathered 6½ dozen; the third day 3 dozen; the fourth day 5 dozen; and on the fifth day they gathered 3½ dozen. Betty and Bill sold the eggs for 60¢ a dozen.

1. How many dozens of eggs did they gather in the five days?_____

2. How many eggs did they gather in the five days? _____

3. How much money did they get for the eggs? _____

4. How much of the money could they keep for themselves?_____

5. How much money did Grandma get?_____

Fill the blanks with the right word or words to complete the sentences.

1. The children arrived at Grandma's on _____

   _____.

2. Before daylight the children heard the _____

   of a_____.

3. _____ seemed happiest of all.

4. There was a _____ in the barn.

5. Grandma and Grandpa lived on a _____

Sixth-Grade Level

Read the story carefully. Then do the exercises that follow the story.

Lucy Picks Beans

Lucy was so excited she could scarcely sleep. Every hour or two she jumped out of bed to peep at the clock ticking noisily on the shelf. What little sleep she got was filled with dreams of the trip on the truck to the bean field.

Finally the clock alarmed and Lucy sprang out of bed and ran to the bathhouse to get washed up for breakfast. While bathing she listened with nervous excitement to the familiar noises that she was accustomed to hearing each morning. Lucy had longed to go on the trucks to the bean field to pick beans with some of the other girls and boys her age, but each Saturday and holiday for her were usually spent doing the family wash, scrubbing, cleaning, and ironing. But yesterday Pa had said she could go on one of the big trucks to pick beans! At last she could earn the money to buy that new dress she had wanted. She actually could ride to the fields and have her own row of beans to pick all by herself. "How can I wait for the beans to dry off before I start picking!" she thought. She would use one of her tickets to buy her lunch from the sandwich wagon which would be waiting in the field. She could join her friends in their competition to see who could pick the most hampers of beans. She just knew that she could pick faster.

Lucy could not hide the eagerness she felt when she thought of all these things. She rushed back to the house and ate her breakfast so hurriedly that her mother exclaimed, "Lucy, slow down, your pa won't let the truck leave you." Lucy almost choked on the grits which she was crowding into her mouth so fast that her jaws were bulging on either side. When she did finish her breakfast at last, Lucy ran to the door before the truck turned the corner which led to their house. She bounded on the truck so fast she nearly lost the sole of her shoe in the haste. She was on at last with the other gang of pickers and away they went to the bean fields laughing and shouting to each other as they passed. Of all the others Lucy was the happiest picker aboard.

Place a number before each of the following sentences to show the order they occurred in the story.

_____ Lucy heard the familiar noises as she was washing for breakfast.

_____ She was too excited to eat.

_____ At last they were off to the fields.

_____ When the clock alarmed she sprang out of bed.

_____ Lucy was too excited to sleep soundly.

Divide the following words into syllables:

struggle_____

excitement_____

familiar_____

accustom_____

bounded_____

Write a sentence in your own words telling the main idea of the first paragraph.

Write a short paragraph telling what you think happened to Lucy that day. (Use the back of this sheet of paper.)

Lucy picked 1½ hampers before lunch and 4½ hampers after lunch. She was paid 80¢ a hamper for picking. She spent 24¢ at the sandwich wagon for her lunch.

1. How many hampers did Lucy pick?_____

2. How much money did she receive?_____

3. How much money did she have after buying her lunch?_____

4. The dress will cost Lucy $5.10. How much more money will she need to buy the dress?_____

5. Lucy and her 5 other friends together picked 30 hampers of beans. What part of the beans did Lucy pick?_____

6. Did Lucy win the contest for picking the most beans?_____

Can you solve these problems?

23	46	57	68	95	79	74
x 3	x 4	x 6	x 7	x 8	x 9	x 5

$5)\overline{754}$ $34)\overline{6368}$ $240)\overline{960}$ $678)\overline{91,099}$

Can you change these fractions to percentages and decimals?

½ _____% _____

¼ _____% _____

¾ _____% _____

attainment, be available in every classroom; that the child first be given an easy exercise, with difficulty increased gradually; that these diagnostic exercises never be referred to as tests; and that they be used repeatedly as the child progressed in his schoolwork.[3]

These diagnostic exercises checked the child's ability to use initial consonants; use consonant blends; read orally on the respective grade levels; read silently on the respective grade levels; comprehend materials read; solve problems involving the fundamental processes in arithmetic; write, both cursive and manuscript; spell at the respective grade levels; and express himself in written composition.

To determine a child's attainment level in arithmetic he was asked to solve problems selected from the review exercises in various arithmetic texts. Many of the teachers prepared mimeographed sheets of these selected problems on several grade levels, and a "buddy" often assisted the child in working on the sheets. These review exercises served as informal diagnostic procedures as well as teaching devices.

A check on the child's spelling was handled similarly. Lists of words were selected from the review pages of the spelling texts. After directing the child to spell orally or to write the words, the teacher began with the easiest words and gradually increased their difficulty until the child reached the level at which he needed instruction.

From a study of these specially prepared diagnostic exercises, the teachers were not only able to determine the child's attainment levels in the basic skill subjects, but also to identify many of the gaps in his learning.

An oral reading diagnostic procedure was used to determine a child's attainment level in reading. Teachers modified this method depending on probable reading interest and attainment and on the classroom situation. The child read privately to the teacher from a set of basic readers, or special exercises prepared for this purpose. First, he read a very easy selection orally, which the teacher was certain he could read without difficulty. Selections gradually increased in difficulty until he read from material on which he consistently missed one word out of twenty. This level was considered his reading attainment level, and instruction was begun at this point. While the child read, the teacher observed and recorded his oral reading habits, such as pointing to words, inserting words, miscalling simple words, omitting words, and his approach to figur-

---

[3] *A Guide to the Education of Agricultural Migratory Children, op. cit.,* p. 63-78 and *Working with Migrant Children in Our Schools,* p. 36-37 and Appendix II.

ing out unfamiliar words. Usually, in order to get some idea of his comprehension skills, she asked a series of questions or used a prepared list of questions to which he wrote the answers. Note was made of the type of questions with which he had difficulty.

During this initial reading period, the teacher gave the child selections to read silently while she checked on comprehension. She observed and recorded such silent reading habits as lip moving, eye sweep, and reading rate. A sample of the inventory sheet on which these reading difficulties were recorded is on p. 68.

STUDY OF SCHOOL RECORDS AND REPORTS

When a migrant child enrolled in school, inquiry was made about a school record or report card. The child was commended for bringing any type of report, and the importance of carrying a school record was pointed out to him. He was shown a copy of the school report which would be given to him when he withdrew, and he was encouraged to inform his teacher of his date of withdrawal so he could receive this report. The child's parents were given the same information, either during home visits or by informal notes and letters of welcome.

Unfortunately, most school reports which children brought with them were of little value in their placement. The information often was either inadequate or misleading. Some children brought transfer records which gave only identification information. When this information was accurate, it was helpful in enrolling and placing the child in a classroom. But it gave no information on the child's attainment levels in his school subjects, and, therefore, was of little value to the classroom teacher. By the time the principal received an acknowledgment in answer to a request for further information, either the teacher had identified the child's instructional needs or the child had already withdrawn from school. Many brought the traditional school report cards. The information they provided was often misleading. Either the reports designated a given grade level with marks or grades indicating that the child had done satisfactory work, and with no reference to the fact that the child's performance level was below the grade designated, or the reports recorded only unsatisfactory and failing grades with no explanation for such marks or the causes of failure. Often, school reports designated first-grade placement for older and more physically mature boys and girls.

Four Spanish-speaking brothers who were small for their ages— seven, eight, ten, and twelve—arrived at one school in November.

INVENTORY OF ORAL READING DIFFICULTIES

NAME	Read-Level	Voice	Points to words	Calls one word at time	Word Attack	Omits, Miscalls words	Punctuation	Physical Obs.	Comprehension
Doe, Bill	1—	high shrill	x	x	spells	on no		squints eyes	poor
Jones, Tom	5—	natural			pictures context				fair

INVENTORY OF SILENT READING DIFFICULTIES

NAME	Read-Level	Moves lips	Moves head	Poor Posture	Interest in Read-Books	Reads until finished	Type question giving trouble	Rate of reading	Comprehension
Doe, Bill	1—	x	x		none	—	details	slow 25	60
Jones, Tom	5—	x			little	x	inference	80	60

According to reports which the three older boys brought, each of them had been enrolled in first grade, and all had been in the same classroom during the previous year. The younger brother had never gone to school. After conferring with the teachers, the principal placed the two younger boys in the first-grade classroom, the ten-year-old in the second, and the twelve-year-old in the third. She commented, "I am ashamed not to place them higher, but this is the best we can do for them now since none of them speak English. But in each of the classrooms there are a few Spanish-speaking children who are about their same size, and I am sure they are better off than to be placed in a classroom where we do not have any Spanish-speaking children."

The usual school report has a space for comments by teachers. Either this space was blank or remarks were written such as, "John is a nice little boy and we have enjoyed having him with us," "Mary is not good in her schoolwork, but she is a sweet child," or "Charles is lazy and does not try in school," obviously of no value in the placement of a child in school.

Reports Can Be Valuable

Most helpful, when received, were informal notes and other illustrative examples of children's past work. One teacher wrote about a nine-year-old, third-grade child:

Mary has made rapid progress these past two months with us. She now reads on second-grade level and has good comprehension, but has difficulty in recalling details. (We use the Scott-Foresman texts for our basal reading program.) According to our program she spells on low second-grade level. I find that she needs help with the initial consonant sounds and the simple consonant blends. I feel that she is ready for more concentration on her spelling, since she is much interested in learning these sounds and frequently tries to spell other more difficult words from the written work on the blackboard and the children's experience records. She can do the regular third-grade arithmetic which we give our children. She seems to have the basic concept of all numbers through 20, reads and writes numbers to 100, and can count by 2's, 5's, and 10's to 100. She loves to make number stories, and we have encouraged stories about her travel and work experiences. Enclosed is a sample of her arithmetic work and her writing which was done this week. I feel that she needs more practice in manuscript writing before she makes the transition to cursive. She knows the correct formation of all the letters, but makes them very slowly. I have been helping her to learn to write on one space, as the example illustrates. She takes pride in doing all her work neatly and accurately.

Mary is a very timid and withdrawing child—we can understand why easily when we realize that she has traveled from school to school, etc.— but we feel that we have helped her to overcome much of this. Now, she works and plays well with the other children. In fact, she has several close friends. The group is giving her a little farewell party. Her parents

have not been able to pay for the school lunches, but I find them interested
in Mary's school progress and appreciative of all we have done for Mary. I
have talked with her mother several times, and have visited her home on
two occasions. According to our regular school health checks, Mary's hearing and vision are normal. She has colds frequently, and we have secured
vitamins for her. I hope that these comments will help you to understand
her needs better. . . .

Both the Palm Beach and Northampton school systems kept
cumulative records on children, and upon enrollment such records
were begun for the migrant children. In the event any migrant
child returned to the same school, teachers found these records
valuable in placing him. When a returning child brought no report,
even after having been away from the school two years, the principal
referred to the cumulative record in order to get information for
classroom placement. Usually this reference resulted in the placement of a child in a classroom two years more advanced than
his previous enrollment.

As the Project continued, an increasing number of migrant children brought school records and an increasing number informed
teachers of withdrawal so that they could take their school reports
with them. Teachers reported that the records began to contain
information that was valuable in placing and teaching the child.

Joe, a 12-year-old migrant boy, enrolled in school in November.
Since he had not attended this school before and had no kind of
school record, the principal spent time talking with him to determine in which classroom to place him. She learned that his
schooling had been very irregular and that he had not been to
school at all that year. He would need instruction on the primary
level, yet he was physically mature and needed to be with boys
of his own age group. Since there were some boys about his size
and age in the fifth grade, the principal decided that Joe would
be able to adjust more readily and do his best work in this fifth-
grade classroom.

He was welcomed into the classroom, and told by his teacher,
"We need a tall boy like you because we have no one who can
place our material on the top of the bulletin boards." A "buddy"
escorted Joe about the classroom, and he was free to explore and
work with any materials which interested him.

During the first day Joe was given some sample arithmetic problems to do. The first sheet consisted of very simple addition and
subtraction combinations which he solved rapidly. Their difficulty
was increased gradually until the teacher found where to begin
instruction in arithmetic. From these diagnostic sheets, she learned
that he knew his addition and subtraction facts, but was weak in
multiplication. He could add and subtract simple fractions, seemed

to have the basic concept of the simpler fractions, and could solve the written problems involving these processes if the teacher assisted him in reading the problems. He liked arithmetic best and enjoyed doing these exercises.

The first two days he was not placed in any reading group, but encouraged to "browse" in the library corner and to choose books which he though he would like to read. The teacher observed that he consistently chose very easy books and seemed to prefer books about drag lines and engines. Selecting books in which he would be interested, and using the oral reading diagnostic procedure, she found that reading instruction for him must begin on the low second-grade level, that he had very little confidence in himself when it came to reading, and that he needed review on all the primary reading skills which precede the second-grade reading level. She discovered also that he would do his best work if permitted to read selections from books relating to his interest rather than from the basal reading texts. His "buddy" helped Joe to check an interest inventory sheet, through which the teacher learned that Joe loved to whittle with a pocket knife and could carve beautifully. During the first week, under the teacher's direction he contributed a carved totem pole to the hobby shelf.

Organization for instruction

The curriculum offered in each school attended by migrants was essentially the same for them as for the resident children. However, the variety of their backgrounds and the irregularity of their attendance required modifications if they were to be taught successfully. These modifications included periods for individual instruction, small group instruction, and periods for the review of essential material.[1] In addition, a helping teacher program was established in one of the school systems, the summer educational enrichment program and the program for exceptional children were extended in the other school system, and one faculty initiated a cooperative plan of teaching.

PROVIDING INDIVIDUAL INSTRUCTION

Individual instruction in reading, spelling, writing, language, arithmetic, as well as in other subjects, was given, and additional exercises were provided for the child to take home for independent study. Frequently, the "buddy" or other children assisted the migrant child in supervised study at school.

Even though a child received individual help from his teacher, he would share in classroom activities with his group as much as possible. Every effort was made to help him feel that he was a regular participating member of the class and not isolated or different because of his need for special help.

Lavonne, nine years old, entered school during the last week of October. Her school experience was limited to a special six-week summer school for migrants during the previous year. She was placed in a third-grade classroom, and the teacher gave her indi-

[1] Special material for Spanish-speaking children is included in Appendix III, p. 134-36.

vidual instruction on the first-grade level. She participated with
the other children in the regular classroom activities of sharing
periods, library periods, music, art, and rhythmic activities, and in
the physical education and play periods. Within a few days some
classmates became interested in her, and, under supervision of
the teacher, took turns in helping her with reading and number
work.

The teacher encouraged and capitalized on all of Lavonne's oral
contributions to the group and often used her contributions to develop an experience story which was shared by all the children.
Lavonne's basic number concept soon was comparable to the third-
grade level, and the teacher assisted her in the reading and solving
of abstract problems so that she could do arithmetic with the class.

"Lavonne improved rapidly and was a happy member of the
group," the teacher reported. "She stayed with us 40 days, and
when she left she could write manuscript legibly . . . write her name
and other identification information without a copy . . . read independently from low first-grade material, and . . . do the regular
third-grade arithmetic with a little help with reading."

A 15-year-old migrant boy entered junior high school and was
enrolled in a seventh-grade social studies section. He was retarded
academically, overdeveloped physically, known as a "bully," and
did not want to attend school. Informed by the principal of the
boy's problems, the teacher welcomed him into the class, permitted
him to choose the place he would like to sit, and arranged a time
for a private conference with him that day.

During the class and before and after school, the teacher helped
the boy with his personal problems, and assisted him with his
social studies assignments. He obtained reading material at a lower
level of difficulty on the topics being studied and helped the boy
organize the information so that he could contribute to the class
discussion. He arranged for him to participate in special class
projects, individually and in cooperation with other members of
the class. Both the teacher and boy were pleased with the results.
The teacher wrote, "He stayed in school and seemed to enjoy social
studies. He was no disciplinary problem and learned to work well
with the other members of the class. He made progress in his reading and writing skills and was able to pass the course."

FLEXIBLE ORGANIZATION OF SMALL GROUPS

Once teachers determined the academic ability of the children,
they organized small groups in the skill subjects at different levels

of proficiency. For the most part, these instructional groups were organized on the basis of the reading and arithmetic attainment levels of the children. Teachers found that most migrant children were more advanced in arithmetic than in reading, spelling, and language, and that they tended to perform at about the same level in the three language arts areas. Groups were flexible; they were reorganized frequently and children were moved to succeedingly higher levels as rapidly as possible. Often, migrant children were members of two reading or arithmetic groups simultaneously.

Both school systems followed a developmental basal reading program, and the migrant child, like all children, was given basic reading instruction on his level of attainment. But, with large numbers of children entering and withdrawing from a classroom, it was necessary to reorganize groups frequently.

In addition to group work in the individual classrooms, there were instances in which the school faculty planned to teach cooperatively in order to give special instruction to small groups of children.

Late in November, two Spanish-speaking migrant boys, 14 and 15 years old, enrolled in the seventh grade. They told the principal that they had been promoted to the eighth grade, but due to the language barrier and their irregular attendance they preferred to be placed in the seventh grade. During an initial conference, the principal learned that the boys could read English fairly well, but that they had an inadequate understanding of the material read and that they spoke very little correct English. The principal made plans for the boys to have additional help with their English conversation and with comprehension of English materials, and a daily 30-minute period was scheduled. The principal or a teacher met with the boys three days a week and members of the student council met with them two days a week. The principal reported, "Both boys liked school and were accepted by the entire student body."

Three primary teachers agreed to remain after school 30 minutes each day to help children with their reading. Approximately 20 migrants, whose reading levels ranged from nonreaders through grade 3, participated. At the end of the school term, after six months, most of the children improved so much that they could read material at their age and grade level.

CLASS PERIODS SCHEDULED FOR REVIEW

Many teachers, especially in the high schools, scheduled class periods for drill on basic skills and review of critical information which the migrant children had missed because of late entrance. These class periods, given over to carefully planned weekly reviews, enabled many to make up back work and to show satisfactory progress. Often, these review periods were supplemented by periods of individual assistance by the teacher.

Immediately following the Christmas holidays, two native Spanish-speaking girls, 15 and 16 years old, enrolled in a ninth-grade English class. They had attended school in another state only one week during that school term. They spoke English well, and were much interested in learning. The class was studying the mechanics of grammar, and the teacher arranged review periods in which the entire class was involved. The girls remained after school for individual help, and the teacher checked the additional practice exercises she had given them to do independently. They made a passing mark on the regular unit test, and continued to make satisfactory progress in English.

THE HELPING TEACHER PROGRAM

The special needs of the migrant children required more teachers for working with individuals and small groups. An experimental project, inaugurated in September 1955 in three Northampton County schools and continuing throughout the duration of the Project, was developed for the purpose of relieving overcrowded classrooms, especially when migrant children were in school during the fall months, and for demonstrating better techniques in teaching the children. Four helping teachers, one to work in each of two schools and two for the third school, were selected by the school board.

In each of two classrooms the helping teacher taught half days, assisting the homeroom teacher who had day-long responsibility for the children. Since teachers recognized the need for additional emphasis on language arts, the helping teachers worked specifically in this area. They also devoted time to arithmetic and assisted the faculty with the selection and use of teaching materials. Children were placed in small groups according to their attainment levels, and schedules were arranged so that the homeroom teacher and the helping teacher each had responsibility for teaching certain groups reading, language, writing, spelling, and arithmetic.

The first two weeks of school each year were given over to a study of the children. The helping teacher interviewed each child and diagnosed his reading needs. She recorded information concerning the interests and background of each child, his instructional reading level, reading difficulties, and specific needs for instruction. The homeroom teacher gave children review exercises and informal check-up tests in spelling, arithmetic, and language. Together, they studied available school records and conferred with the children's former teachers.

Arithmetic and reading groups were organized, and daily programs were devised in each of the two classrooms. The helping teacher taught the three lower-attainment groups in each of the two classrooms, and the homeroom teacher taught the higher-attainment groups. A developmental reading program was provided through the use of the basal reading texts. This program was supplemented by the use of experience reading, directed reading from other books, and independent reading of library books. The teachers developed and used independent reading activities to meet specific needs of individual children in the language arts.

The instructional groups were flexible, and children were moved from group to group according to progress. Every effort was made to help each child, both migrant and nonmigrant, feel that he was an integral part of the total classroom group. Opportunities were given him to share and to participate with all children in the classroom.

In order to strengthen the program as it developed, reports of progress, problems, and activities were given each month.[2] In an early progress report, these observations were made:

1. Informal grouping of seats provided opportunity for small groups to work together while the teacher worked with another group
2. Study plans and activities listed on the board guided children to work on their own levels independently
3. Experience reading charts motivated reading and developed interest in the language arts
4. When given the opportunity, migratory children made unique contributions on the growing of agricultural crops and the states and communities in which they had lived
5. Children were eager to show their work to visitors and to tell them about their classrooms
6. Emotional climate of classrooms was improved. Children seemed to enjoy their schoolwork, and some children developed improved attitudes toward school.

[2] As an outgrowth of the first year of the program, helping teachers, homeroom teachers, the supervisor, and the Project Supervisor developed a curriculum bulletin outlining a developmental reading program, *A Guide for the Teaching of Reading, op. cit.*

A COOPERATIVE TEACHING PROGRAM

The faculty of one school, recognizing that so many of their migrant pupils could not write legibly and that they seemed to value good handwriting, arranged through a cooperative teaching plan to give special emphasis to this skill. The fourth-grade teacher, who had been successful in teaching children handwriting, assumed the responsibility of leadership for the program. Teachers met informally to improve their own handwriting and to plan their individual classroom programs of writing instruction. One period a week, while another teacher took over her class, the fourth-grade teacher gave special instruction to the children in the third-, fifth-, and sixth-grade classrooms.

During these exchange periods, the activities in the fourth-grade classrooms included viewing and discussing educational films and slides; selecting and reading library books; discussing current events; reading stories and books independently; and practicing reading, spelling, and arithmetic skills individually. Frequently, the principal arranged to teach the fourth-graders, thereby relieving the classroom teacher to observe, or to participate in, the special writing instructions for her pupils. The teachers followed up each instructional period with writing activities which provided additional practice for the students.

All the children made marked improvement in their handwriting. Parents commented frequently on how well their children could write, and the easily observable evidence that they were "learning in school" helped to establish better relationships between parents and the school.

AN EDUCATIONAL ENRICHMENT PROGRAM

A summer program was provided by the Palm Beach County Board of Public Instruction to serve children, some of whose parents were migrants remaining in a labor housing center during the summer. Two teachers were employed to direct the project, which was established as a part of the regular Summer Educational Enrichment Program and had the cooperation of a number of agencies. Several classrooms, a tin shelter which was equipped for preparing and serving meals, and the school grounds were made ready for the program. The housing authority and local civic clubs provided additional recreation equipment and supplies. The Christian Ministry to Migrants arranged for two of their trained workers to assist the two directors full-time. The county demonstration agent helped with the homemaking and arts and crafts activities from time to time. One of the parents in the camp used his truck to transport groups of children to the swimming pool. He made four trips weekly. The housing authority purchased the necessary gasoline.

The program provided a balance of indoor and outdoor activities: sports and games—softball, volley ball, table tennis, badminton, relays, track and field contests, and bicycling; arts and crafts— painting, drawing, finger painting, puppet making, poster making, weaving, and working with clay and bamboo; music—marching, singing, folk games, and square dancing; library—free reading, story telling, and film showings; and homemaking—making tea towels and curtains, crocheting, food preparation and serving, and discussions on table manners and health. The program was in operation five days a week from 8 a.m. until 5 p.m. for six weeks, with the younger children coming mornings and the older children, afternoons.

Approximately 150 children were enrolled, and the average daily attendance was one of the highest in the county. Special programs and events were arranged for the parents each week. The principal reported that juvenile delinquency decreased in the camp and that the summer program was at least one contributing factor.

A PROGRAM FOR EXCEPTIONAL CHILDREN

The Palm Beach County exceptional child program was adjusted so that the maximum number of migrant children could partici- pate. They were included in the curriculum adjustment classes, in the special services for speech improvement, in the Royal Palm School at Pahokee,[3] and in the classes for homebound children. The three schools having special rooms for curriculum adjustment classes continually reorganized groups in order to provide special remedial reading instruction. Both resident and migrant children improved in reading proficiencies to the point where they could make satisfactory progress in their regular classrooms, and they were replaced by other children. Those assigned to the remedial reading classes received one hour daily of special instruction which was designed in terms of their reading attainment levels and their special weaknesses and problems. In addition, teachers made and recorded careful observations, held private interviews with children and their parents, and reported their findings to the classroom teachers.

---

[3] This school serves physically handicapped and mentally retarded children in the Glades area.

John, age 13 years, entered school in February and was assigned to a special remedial reading class because he was a nonreader. By May, 15 weeks later, he was reading at the second-grade level.

Mary, age 13 years, had a reading level of 3.3 (level normally expected for a child during the third month of the third grade) when she was placed in a special reading group at the end of September. By May, her reading level was 5.1, an improvement of one full year and eight months in eight months.

Cortez, a 14-year-old Spanish-speaking boy, entered school in February and was assigned to a special reading class. He could read English from first-grade material. By the close of school in June, four months later, his reading level was 2.9, a gain of a full year.

Curriculum adaptation

To help children acquire basic skills and develop their potentialities, modifications were made in the school curriculum by adapting learning material to the children's attainment level, by drawing from their own experiences, and by developing material for classroom use from all available sources to increase interest and facilitate learning.

USE OF CHARTS

Experience records, in the form of booklets and charts, were drawn from different subject areas, from the routine organization for living and working together, and from school activities and functions. These records served as a principal reference source to which the children could refer for writing and spelling words and for the correct use of capital letters and marks of punctuation:

1. A summary chart listing important facts studied and learned
2. A daily news story of the current classroom happenings
3. Charts of correct English forms for letters, thank-you notes, business letters, and check-writing
4. "Reminder charts" with schedules for immunization and clinic programs, procedure for checking books from the library, and announcements of special school events
5. Charts with safety rules and directions for fire drills
6. Charts listing directions on how to use the dictionary, the encyclopedia, and other reference books
7. Charts recording the responsibilities of individuals and committees
8. Charts of classroom plans for a day or for a unit or special school project
9. Charts listing standards for oral and silent reading as set up by the children

10. Charts recording daily accounts of science observations, experiments, temperature, and weather.

This is illustrative of a summary chart:
We learned these things about the origin of beans today:
Beans first grew in Eastern Asia.
Beans are one of the oldest crops we know.
Beans were first grown in America by the Indians.
These Indians lived in South America.

A chart developed by the children who had been up-state was used to teach the correct use of capital letters. Children illustrated it by placing appropriate pictures in each of the center spaces:

Beans	....	beans
Strawberries	....	strawberries
Indians	....	
Ferry	....	ferry
United States Capitol	....	
Bridges	....	bridges
Cheriton Labor Camp	....	
Irish potatoes	....	
Sweet potatoes	....	sweet potatoes

An outline chart was used to help children learn to write and spell their names, addresses, and other identification information:

My name is_____   I go to the_____School
My mother's name is_____   The principal is_____
My father's name is_____   My teacher is_____
We live in the_____   I am in the _____grade
My house number is_____

I live in_____
Pahokee is in_____
Palm Beach County is in_____
I attend the_____
The principal is_____
My parents are_____
Our address is_____

EXPERIENCE READING

In the development of basic concepts and skills in the language arts, teachers supplemented textual content with experience reading. In fact, some teachers used only the experience reading approach until the children developed sufficient vocabulary to read from books which were comparable to their levels of interest. In

many situations, children recorded their stories in individual booklets which they illustrated and reread from time to time. Most
teachers transferred these stories to large charts and displayed
them in the classrooms. Others, using loose-leaf binders, made
books from collections of these experience reading charts.

An experience reading story was developed by fifth-grade migrant
children:

> We live in the Glades area of Palm Beach County, Florida.
> Here we grow many vegetables.
> There are beans, celery, corn, lettuce, and many others.
> We grow twenty-three (23) kinds of vegetables.
> The fresh vegetables are shipped by trains and trucks to
>   the Northern states.
> They call the Glades, "The Winter Vegetable Garden of
>   the World."

ORIGINAL MATERIALS

Some teachers developed original materials based on a current
interest or some experience which the migrant children had shared,
and adjusted the material to their level of performance. Many of
these were for use in reading and the language arts. Examples
of such stories and exercises follow on p. 86-90.

"Here We Go Traveling" (see p. 91) was a game used for
practicing number facts. On a heavy sheet of cardboard, a continuous line is drawn to illustrate the highway traveled from Belle Glade
to New York. "Stops"—spaces on the diagram—are scattered along
the highways at which the player must stop. To travel on, he must
answer correctly an arithmetic, vocabulary, or spelling problem
given by the teacher. Each player is given a colored marker to indicate the distance he has traveled. The game proceeds as each
player takes turns traveling and answering the problem given for
each stop. If he answers correctly, he moves on to the next stop.
If he misses, he must go back to the previous stop. The player
who reaches New York first wins the game.

Teachers found that story problems which involved reading content as well as the basic number concepts were valuable:

> Joe and Sue picked beans Saturday. Joe picked 4 hampers of beans and
> Sue picked 3 hampers. How many hampers did they pick together?
>
> The man paid them 60¢ for picking one hamper. How much did Sue make?
> How much money did Joe make? How much did they make together? [1]

---

[1] Text continued on p. 92.

EXPERIENCE READING STORIES

Johnny Picks Cotton

Johnny is going to the field.
Johnny is going to help Father.
He is going to help pick cotton.
Johnny likes to pick cotton.
He likes to help Father.
Father and Johnny put on a sack
to hold the cotton.
Father and Johnny start to work.
Johnny works hard.
Father works hard.
The sun is hot.
Johnny looks at the field.
The cotton looks pretty in the sun.
Father has two full sacks of cotton.
Johnny has one full sack.
It is time to eat.
Father and Johnny go home.
They go home to eat.
Johnny stays home now.
Johnny stays to help mother.
Father will pick more cotton.
Johnny will help mother.
Johnny can pick more cotton tomorrow.

1. Johnny likes to pick cotton.   Yes   No
2. Johnny does not work hard.   Yes   No
3. Johnny picks all day.   Yes   No

A Dog Show

There was to be a dog show in Osceola Center. It was only for boys and girls. The boy or girl who had the best-trained dog was to get the prize.

Susan Hall had a dog who could do tricks. He knew one good trick and four that were not so good. His best trick was to stand up on his back legs.

Tim Black's dog was the best-looking dog in the show. He could run like the wind when Tim told him to run after a stick and bring it back.

Jim Brown's dog, Buck, would sit, stand, walk, and lie down when Jim gave him the right sign.

"You have to be a very well-trained pet to do all that by signs," said Mr. Hap, the man who was helping the children with the show.

1. The best name for this story is:
   A Trick Dog.   A Running Dog.
   A Good Dog.   At the Dog Show.

2. The number of tricks that Susan's dog could do was:
   one   three   two   five.

3. The one who got the prize was:
   the one with the best-looking dog.
   the one with the best-trained dog.
   the one with a dog who could do tricks.

4. The dog show was only for:
   boys   children   girls   dogs.

5. The one man who got the prize was:
   Susan   Tim   Buck   Jim.

Can You Find My Name?

I am red. I have green spots.
I am good to eat.
You can pick me in Michigan.
What am I?

cotton

I am round and white.
I am soft.
You cannot eat me.
You can pick me in Arkansas.
What am I?

strawberry

I am brown outside.
I am white inside.
I have eyes, but I cannot see.
You can eat me.
You can pick me in Virginia.
What am I?

bean

I am green.
I am long.
I am good to eat.
You can pick me in Florida.
What am I?

potato

a	b
c_t	_ird
_pple	_eet
_c_r	_oat
_x	_read

St-tr-fl- gr	Sh-fr-bl-st
_awberries	_elters
_actor	_uit
_orida	_ueberries
_apes	_ar

13 − 11 = ?

16 ÷ 4 = ?

12 − 7 = ?

6 × 9 = ?

11 × 5 = ?

13 + 6 = ?

11 − 4 = ?

20 ÷ 5 = ?

8 × 1 = ?

17 − 8 = ?

Joe spent 75¢ of his money to buy a new shirt. He gave his teacher $1.25 to pay for his school lunches the next week. How much money did he have left?

Last week their mother picked beans and earned five times as much as Joe and Sue together earned on Saturday. How much did she earn? How many hampers of beans did she pick during the week?

Arithmetic assignments involved actual experiences of the children and their parents. In one assignment a road map was used:

1. A. Chart route from Michigan to the Glades.
   B. How far was the trip?
   C. How long did you actually travel?
   D. What was the average distance traveled daily? Per hour?
   E. At an average of 11 miles per gallon, how many gallons of gas were consumed?
   F. If the average cost of gas per gallon was 31¢, what was the total gas bill for the trip?

2. A bean grader earns 65¢ an hour.
   A packing supervisor earns $1.05 an hour.
   A header earns 90¢ an hour.

Each works the following number of hours during the week:

Sun.	Mon.	Tues	Wed.	Thurs.	Fri.	Sat.
9 hrs.	15 hrs.	8 hrs.	11 hrs.	14 hrs.	18 hrs.	16 hrs.

Find and compare the weekly wage of each person.

Other arithmetic exercises follow on p. 93-96.

THE CREATIVE ARTS

Migrant children were encouraged to write about their experiences, dramatize original plays, and interpret orally selections from stories. They participated in singing, and learned to play musical instruments. They were encouraged to draw, paint, play rhythmic games, and dance.

A fourth-grade teacher arranged for her 40 pupils, of whom approximately one half were migrants, to have an opportunity for creative dramatic expression through the use of a common experience. The teacher was a newcomer to the area, and told the class that she was unfamiliar with the bean harvesting process, and that she wanted to learn about it. Making careful preplans, she initiated and led the children in a discussion on bean harvesting, from which she learned that all but one of the children had picked beans [2]

---

[2] Text continued on p. 97.

ARITHMETIC EXERCISES

Grade Three

I.

Count by 2's, 5's, and 10's to 100.

II.

Add: 32   40   Subtract: 38   38¢
         +4   +7   −5   −5¢
         ___   ___   ___   ___

III.

Jack helped his Daddy catch fish.

Jack caught 3

His Daddy caught 8

How many   did they catch in all?

IV.

We had 10 gifts in the gift box.
We gave our new friends 8 gifts this week.
We have_____gifts left.

V.

Tom had 10 pieces of bubble gum.
He divided it with Jerry.
How many did each get?

Grade Four

1. Your brother works 7 hours in the packing house on Monday, 8 hours on Tuesday, and 5 hours on Wednesday. How many hours does he work this week?

2. Your father picks 15 hampers of peppers, your mother picks 10 hampers, and you pick 8 hampers on Friday. How many crates does your family pick together?

3. Your father earns $20 per week.
    Your mother earns $15 per week.
    Your brother earns $18 per week.
    How much does your family earn together?

4. How many hampers will you have if you pick 3 hampers of beans on Monday and 2 hampers on Tuesday? How much money will you earn if they pay 60¢ per hamper?

Grade Five

1.

1 minute   = _____seconds

1 hour   = _____minutes

1 foot   = _____inches

6 oranges = _____what part of a dozen_____

2.

The teacher reads the following numbers and pupil writes the number correctly:

    1,560;   321,961;   999,100;   89,121

3.

It took a family 2 weeks and 3 days to make the trip from Michigan to Florida. How many days were they traveling?

4.

How much will the family spend for milk if they buy 54 half pints for $.09 each?

5.

Add: 627   Copy in columns, add and check:
         491
         373      $.75 + $1.75 + $4.00
         846
         538

6.

Divide and check:

    $6\overline{)\,54\,}$ $7\overline{)\,56.35\,}$

Grade Six

1. Place comma in the correct place in the figures below:

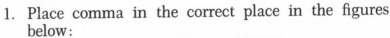

999100 — 866332

2. 627
    491
    373
    846
   +538

3. 7630
   −6974

4. Multiply:
   583                    $52.09
   x67   x85

5. Divide: 48) 1546   49) 3793

6. Reduce the following whole or mixed numbers:

   2/2   2/4   4/4   5/4   9/4   10/4   6/8

7. Add:
   (½ + ¼)   (5/10 + 2/5)   (⅛ + ¼ + ½)

8. Subtract:
   5/15   ½   4 2/3
   −2/15   −¼   −2 1/3

9. Express in decimal form:
            1/2 of a dollar is_____
            1/4 of a dollar is_____

10. Draw a circle—divide into sixths

11. Which is larger, 1/10 or 1/5?

and that they were thoroughly familiar with the field operations for bean harvesting.

The class agreed that they would like to dramatize the process for her. She explained that she wanted them to act out everything that happened during the day from the time the workers were picked up by the truck at the loading zone to the time they returned to the loading zone. They chose players and formed a committee to arrange the room into the bean field, loading zone, and "pay-off" station.

The play began with the whole class assembled around the loading zone. The foreman said, "All out to the bean field—paying 80¢ a hamper today. Load up, and let's go."

The jeep driver with the foreman beside him led the way, followed by the truck drivers, the pickers, and the girl who operated the sandwich wagon. The drivers traveled around the classroom twice, then stopped at the back to unload at the bean field. The foreman said, "Get you a row. When the beans are dry, start picking." The pickers scattered along the back of the room in small groups: some sat on the floor and others stood talking together. Then, the foreman called out, "Okay, the beans are dry. Start picking."

The luggers passed out cardboard cartons for hampers and the bean pickers moved up and down the rows, some stooping and others on their knees. As a picker filled his hamper with beans, the checker gave him a ticket of red construction paper. The luggers moved back and forth to the truck, carrying cartons, emptying the beans into large sacks, and returning empty hampers to the pickers. A few at a time, they went to the sandwich wagon and exchanged tickets for sandwiches and soft drinks.

The bean picking continued several minutes. The foreman moved about giving directions to the weighers, luggers, and checkers. Then, he raised his hand and called out, "Okay, time to knock off."

Bean pickers moved from the field to the space behind the truck driver, the luggers picked up the hampers, and the trucks returned to the loading zone. The pickers lined up at the pay station ready to receive their money. Each of the pickers stepped up to the "pay-window," and the pay-off man asked, "How many tickets?" After everyone had been "paid off," the foreman announced, "Got plenty of beans to pick tomorrow."

The children enjoyed performing and the teacher was pleased at their spontaneity. As they left for the day, one child said, "Sure did enjoy school today," and another, "I hope you'll let us do this again."

One day during an art period, a seventh-grade teacher observed that Monty, who had been in school only two days, was drawing a picture of a football player. The player was jumping into the air ready to catch the on-coming ball. Recognizing that Monty was doing an unusual job of getting action into his picture, he began talking with him about drawing. He learned that Monty liked to draw "just for fun." Monty told him that he had never had any special art training, and that he had done most of his drawings outside of school. The next day he brought in some drawings to show the class. The children liked his work and gave him the responsibility for making posters to advertise their baseball games.

The teacher showed Monty's collection to the faculty and to the Project Supervisor, and sought suggestions from them on ways he could help Monty to develop his talent for drawing. Monty was transferred to a large high school in West Palm Beach, Florida. A letter of transfer was directed to the principal which included an explanation of his art interest and talent, the activities which the teacher had arranged in order to encourage and develop this talent, and a recommendation that he be placed in an art class.

MATERIALS DEVELOPED FROM PRINTED SOURCES

Throughout the Project, special attention was given to the selection of books and other printed materials which were geared to the interests and experiences of migrant children and which presented a vocabulary comparable to their levels of reading attainment.

Teachers developed instructional materials from printed sources. Pictures, stories, information on special topics, and selected practice exercises and activities were taken from textbooks, workbooks, library books, magazines, and from inexpensive and free materials.

Selected Pictures Served a Variety of Purposes

To develop reading readiness, collections of pictures of fruits, vegetables, animals, ways of traveling, or pictures illustrating a story were placed in separate folders. Each child was given a folder and asked to classify his pictures into two categories, vegetable and fruit; vegetables which mature under the ground and vegetables which mature above the ground; safe animals and dangerous animals; or into three categories, red fruit, yellow vegetable, and green vegetable. Then, he arranged the pictures into proper sequence to illustrate a story.

To supplement textual material, selected pictures served to relate content material from texts more specifically to the experience and background of migrant children.

A group of children were reading a primary book from the basic Scott-Foresman Reading Series. They had discussed how Dick and Jane helped their father and mother. The teacher showed them a picture of a bean field with two children standing near the edge of the field. Immediately, the children recognized another way which Dick and Jane might help since it was a way in which they helped their parents, and they developed a story about the picture:

> Dick and Jane help Mother and Father.
> Dick picks beans.
> Jane picks beans, too.
> See the pretty green beans.
> We like to eat green beans.
> Do you like green beans?

"Cut-up Stories" Provided Material for Practice on Reading Skills

Stories selected to represent the independent reading level or the instructional reading level of the group were taken from two copies of a discarded textbook or library book, pasted to cardboard, cut into sections, and placed in an envelope with the name of the story printed on the outside. The cards were numbered to indicate the sequence of the story or left unnumbered. An envelope was given to a group of children and each child chose a card which he read silently. When cards were not numbered, each child read his portion, and as a group the class placed the story in sequence. The children were encouraged to "tell the story" to an audience by reading each section so that it seemed to those listening they were just "talking to them." Sometimes, teachers prepared follow-up exercises to be written such as, "Find the picture words" or "Find two words that have similar meanings."

Booklets Created Interest in Independent Reading

Stories and articles giving reference information were taken from used texts and library books and bound into booklets with colored construction paper. These booklets were used by children as independent reading to secure supplementary information about a topic being studied. Some teachers selected stories on several reading levels and used the booklet in determining the instructional reading levels of migrant children.

Worksheets Provide Practice on Needed Skills

Sheets of selected exercises and activities relating to the basic skills were taken from workbooks, textbooks, and teachers' manuals, pasted on cardboard, and organized according to subject and level of difficulty. In arithmetic, for example, these worksheets consisted of practice exercises on addition and subtraction facts, multiplication and division of integers, counting money, and telling time. In reading, the worksheets contained exercises on word recognition, vocabulary development, and reading comprehension. The teacher selected an appropriate worksheet for a child to complete independently in order to "practice on the things he had missed." Sometimes, a worksheet was selected for a small group of children to do as a follow-up exercise to an instructional reading or arithmetic period. Each child did his work on a separate sheet of paper which was checked by the teacher, after which the worksheet was returned to the folder or file for further use by others.

MODIFICATIONS IN TEACHING METHODS

Whatever subject is being taught, it is important for the teacher to be flexible in her method of approach. Without preparation or planning in advance, she should be able to place difficult concepts in a context the child will understand or make use of a piece of information a child may share.

During an instructional arithmetic period the teacher recognized that Bill, a fifth-grade migrant boy, was having difficulty understanding common fractions. The group had cut sheets of paper into halves and fourths, but Bill didn't understand the concept. The teacher said, "Bill, look at the two sheets of paper which you have cut into four equal parts and tell me how much one and one-fourth less three-fourths is." The child hesitated. The teacher then said, "Let's think of this in another way. If you had $1.25, which is one and one-fourth dollars, and you gave me 75¢, which is three-fourths of a dollar, how much would you have left?" Immediately Bill responded, "Fifty cents." "From this simple illustration," the teacher wrote, "Bill gained a better understanding of the meaning of fractions." When migrant children have had experience with money, and when relationships to money can be shown, they can reason problems out on the basis of their experiences.

A migrant child brought his teacher a picture of the "Princess Anne," a ferry on which he had crossed the Chesapeake Bay. The teacher made use of the picture by developing a composition about the boat as a group experience:

"Princess Anne" is a large boat which ferries people across the Chesapeake Bay. There are five different boats that cross the Bay several times each day, transporting people to and from Kiptopeke and Little Creek, Virginia. The names of these boats are: Princess Anne, Pocahontas, Delmarva, Northampton, and Accomack. One sees many cars, buses, and trucks from different states on these boats. While crossing on these large boats, people may walk around on the outside deck and view the beautiful Chesapeake Bay. They may watch the barges and other small boats glide across the water. It is about twenty-one miles across the Bay, and it takes one and one-half hours to cross. It is fun to ride on Princess Anne when the waves are quiet.

Twenty-five children, most of whom were migrants, were being instructed in speech improvement by the speech therapist. The teacher reported that "the children were attentive and seemed to enjoy my time with them but they did not actually realize what speech was, and there was no apparent connection made with everyday speech or reading." She decided to dramatize each sound taught with objects which were familiar to the children. For example, to teach the "N" sound (which she called the mosquito sound), she made some hand puppets of a family of mosquitoes and told a story of how "Millie Mosquito learned to hum . . . n . . . n . . . n" while the children manipulated the various puppet characters. To teach the "S" (snake) sound, she had the children dramatize visits to the camp store, where they bought cigarettes, pencils, and scissors, for which they paid six and seven cents. For the "F" (angry cat) sound, she made finger ring puppets to dramatize a poem involving the sounds. She reported, "The group is progressing nicely. . . . They grasp quickly the sounds introduced; they can think of words containing each sound, and are capable of telling where the sound occurs in a word (initial, medial, or final)."

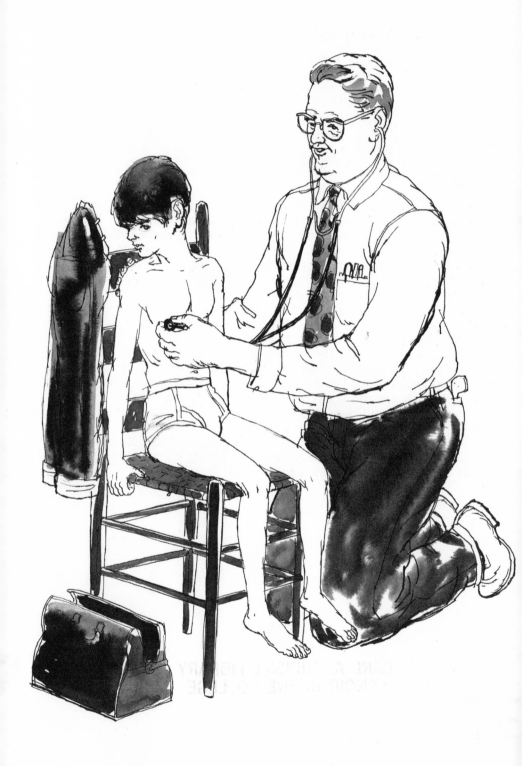

Teaching health

Basic health needs are the same for all children, but the life pattern of the migrant child creates unusual health conditions and, therefore, special needs. Learning about the health conditions of migrant children, providing services to meet their needs, and offering learning experiences which will improve these conditions, with health department assistance, is a responsibility of the schools.

The school health programs in Northampton and Palm Beach counties provided for a school environment designed to insure safe, sanitary, and healthful living conditions, both physically and mentally; learning experiences directed toward the development of good health practices; physical education and recreation suitable to the needs, interests, and physical conditions of the children; and health services sponsored by the county health departments.

To develop a program of health instruction in school, teachers learned about the health conditions and health habits of migrant children. To assemble information, they used informal observations and conversations, tested vision and weight, referred to available health records, and consulted with school nurses.

PERSONAL HYGIENE AND GROOMING

Before entering school, adequate clothing and medical care were among children's immediate needs. Most schools had a supply of clothing available to provide migrants with complete outfits or additional pieces of clothing. In some cases, the teachers bought new clothing for children in their classrooms or furnished them with clothing from their own home or from neighbors and friends.

Two girls, 13 and 14 years old, came to enroll in school. The principal observed that the girls were inadequately and inappropriately clothed, that they were infected with impetigo, and that they were extremely shy and embarrassed. "I began talking with the girls about the places they had lived, and tried in every way to put them at ease," the principal reported, "after which they gave me a note from their mother." The mother had written that the girls had no clothes for school, no money for lunches, and they needed glasses. The principal supplied the girls with clothing and notified the mother that an oculist would examine their eyes the following week. She arranged for the girls to be taken to the health clinic that afternoon. The nurse treated the girls for impetigo and visited the home to counsel the mother about further treatment. The girls entered school the next day. Later, a local church group furnished clothing and food supplies to the entire family, and, through the local Lions Club, glasses were purchased for both girls. During the four months they lived in the area they came to school regularly. They were always clean and took good care of the clothing which had been given to them.

Special lessons were held on good health habits and their importance. Films were shown and demonstrations were given by classroom teachers and nurses on the care of the hair—brushing, shampooing, and styling; the care of the teeth—proper brushing and the use of salt and soda if no dentifrice was available; the care of eyes, ears, and nails; and the care of clothing. Teachers used daily charts on which health habits were checked. "Reminder charts" which called attention to clean clothing, to the use of handkerchiefs or tissues, and to general bodily cleanliness were displayed in classrooms. Teachers, as well as nurses, had private interviews with migrant children about their personal hygiene problems.

Some of the schools arranged for children to take showers while at school through arrangements with physical education teachers and under the supervision of high-school students.

Johnny, seven years old, was unclean and wore dirty clothes. Contacts with the parents by the teacher and nurse were unsuccessful in improving his appearance. The teacher arranged for Johnny to take showers at school. She gave him clean clothing and her husband took him to a barber shop where he received his first professional haircut. Johnny's appearance improved and he enjoyed the showers, but his mother took no responsibility for helping Johnny come to school clean.

Marjie, seven years old, came to school dirty and wearing soiled clothing. The teacher visited her home and found very unsanitary living conditions there. She arranged for a group of high-school girls to give Marjie showers in the physical education department. The girls became interested in Marjie, and, in addition to the baths, they shampooed and cared for her hair, made new clothes for her, and kept her clothing laundered. The teacher writes, "There was a complete change in her personal appearance and personality;

she was one of our happiest pupils, and all the children liked
her. . . . Her shyness was washed away with the dirt. When Marjie
moved on after a few months she cried when leaving school, 'I hate
to leave these good people.' "

FOOD AND NUTRITION

Symptoms of malnutrition among the children made providing
food for them and teaching them about nutrition a necessary part
of the work of the school. Free lunches at school were given to
children when their parents were unable to pay. Schools with no
lunch program usually furnished milk. In two of the larger schools
in Palm Beach County, mid-morning lunches, consisting of fruit
juices, powdered milk, and bread-and-butter sandwiches, were provided for children who were underweight or who seemed listless and
tired. Children looked forward to the food, teachers noticed "fewer
heads drooped to desk tops during the day," and records indicated
that each child gained weight.

When symptoms of malnutrition were observed, teachers contacted the nurse, and usually vitamins were given at school under
the direction of the health department. Most classrooms kept individual records of the changes in children's height and weight. When
children failed to make normal gains in weight they were sent to the
clinic for an examination.

The importance of eating a balanced diet was emphasized through
health lessons, units, and classroom activities. Teachers used slides,
films, dramatizations, charts, and illustrative materials showing
the kinds of food a child should have daily. Special attention was
placed on information about inexpensive foods which were
nutritious.

The teacher observed that Joe, seven years old, seemed sleepy
during the day. His attendance was very irregular, and she was
concerned because he was not making the progress in his schoolwork of which he was capable. He was being given free lunches
at school, but she decided that he needed more food. She arranged
for him to have a large glass of milk each morning when he came
to school. At lunch she checked that he had additional milk and
ate all his food. As a result, she reported, "Joe improved in his
schoolwork. . . . He did not seem listless and sleepy, and was very
active. . . . He grew two inches and gained five pounds in the
three months he was with us."

Shirley, an 11-year-old newcomer, was bringing a 15-cent box
of cookies, a 10-cent bag of potato chips, and a 5-cent bar of

candy to school for lunch each day. The teacher arranged a special health lesson on the need for a balanced diet. She talked with Shirley privately, telling her she was not eating the food a growing girl should have, and that she was spending 30 cents a day when a wholesome lunch in the lunchroom would cost her only 25 cents. Shirley began to eat in the lunchroom and, the teacher wrote, "She seemed very pleased that I had helped her to change to a proper diet."

Migrant children often did not like or would not eat foods served in the school cafeteria with which they were unfamiliar. Special efforts were made to encourage eating a wider variety of foods and enjoying them.

A first-grade teacher arranged a milk party for her class every few weeks. The children helped to make milk from powdered milk to which they added chocolate syrup, mashed bananas, or other fruit. Facts about milk were written on a large chart which was displayed for the party:

Milk is better for boys and girls than Kool-Aid or Coca-Cola.

Milk helps us have strong bones and good teeth.

We should drink three or four glasses of milk a day.

A glass of milk made from powdered milk costs less than
    two cents.

The teacher reported that all children learned to like powdered milk, and that most of them learned to take it without syrup or fruit.

With the cooperation of the luncheon personnel, a teacher planned a tasting party several times a month. Foods were served attractively in small quantities: latticed-sliced carrots, rose-petal radishes, celery bows, and bits of cauliflower; small open sandwiches spread with cheese, peanut butter, jelly, and assorted meats; and reconstituted powdered milk served in colored paper cups with a straw. The teacher reported that "children gradually learned to eat normal-sized servings of all foods tasted and to drink the milk."

A "Two-Bite Club" was formed in which each child was required to take at least two bites of everything on his lunch tray in order to belong to the club. Although all children did not learn to like all foods most learned to enjoy a greater variety.

COMMUNICABLE AND NONCOMMUNICABLE DISEASES

The most common illnesses among migrant children are colds, toothaches, earaches, styes, headaches, and stomach-aches. When a child became ill, the case was reported to the nurse, who determined the cause or arranged for the child to come to the clinic for an examination by the physician.

A newcomer cried and complained of a stomach-ache during the mid-morning period. The teacher felt that the child was unhappy because of the strangeness of a new situation and did everything to comfort him and to help him become adjusted. She noted, though, that he stopped crying after lunch, and seemed content. On the third morning, while talking with him about the kinds of food he had been eating, she learned that his mother went to work early and he was coming to school without breakfast. The teacher took him to the lunchroom where he was given milk and hot oatmeal. His mother was contacted and she arranged for the child to have breakfast before going to school. His crying and stomach-aches ceased.

In addition to these common illnesses and complaints, migrant children frequently have scabies, impetigo, "muck sores," and other skin eruptions. Pediculosis, also, is prevalent. In these situations, the health department's recommendation for treatment was relayed to parents by both nurses and teachers.

Because migrants often missed regularly scheduled immunizations, they contracted communicable diseases more readily than other children. If symptoms of such a disease were noticed, the child was sent to the school infirmary or taken home, if the parents were at home. Teachers continually encouraged children and parents to contact the nurse or go to the clinic in the case of illness. The clinics, too, welcomed the requests of individual migrant families that their children receive immunizations which they had missed.

SANITATION

The need for improved sanitary conditions is a constant problem for most migratory families. The school helped by teaching children to understand and to practice at home basic principles of sanitation. As migrant children associated with classmates, they became familiar with sanitation practices in the use of the bathroom, lunchroom, and playground facilities. By serving on committees they shared in the responsibilities of checking room temperature, ventilation, and lighting; supervising hand washing before lunch time; checking during the lunch period to see that all food was properly discarded; and assisting with the general cleanliness of the classroom, the disposal of waste paper, the care of blackboards, chalk, erasers, and the care of the school ground.

Attention was given in the classroom to home sanitation. Topics discussed were the disposal of waste water and garbage; the importance of obtaining drinking water from a safe source; the use of individual drinking cups and combs; the correct way of washing dishes; the care of food without refrigeration; the care of food while traveling; the extermination of rodents, flies, mosquitoes, and other insects; and the use of disinfectants.

REST, RELAXATION, AND PLAY

Lack of attention to the need for rest in addition to the responsibility of caring for younger children while their parents work create irregular sleeping habits among migrant children. When they do sleep, many children remain in their clothes or underwear, crowded on a bed with other brothers and sisters.

Teachers recommended to children that they have an adequate amount of sleep each night, and that they wear comfortable clothing for sleeping. They advised 10 hours of sleep for children of elementary-school age and, since the majority of migrant children did not have the conventional gowns or pajamas for sleeping, they advised sleeping in a clean, loose garment. In the Glades area of Palm Beach County, the teachers explained that windows should be kept closed at night, an important health rule in the severely damp climate of that area of the country.

Since migrant children have so little opportunity for rest and relaxation, schools provide a physical education program and clubs for them to join. Magazines, games, and toys usually can be borrowed overnight by the children for use at home.

SAFETY AND FIRST AID

Teachers who are familiar with the home life of migrant children know that there are many hazards to which they are subjected daily. Safety instruction included lessons in the use of matches, kerosene, and gas burners; the proper disposal of rubbish around the home to eliminate cuts and punctures while playing; and safety measures while playing at home and while walking and driving on the highways.

Nevertheless, instruction at school did not prevent many children from receiving bruises, cuts, or punctures from nails, glass, and tins while playing unsupervised at home. Teachers administered first aid and taught the children how to use the first-aid kit. They emphasized the importance of having a well-furnished first-aid kit accessible at home and during travels.

MENTAL HEALTH

In Palm Beach County, the services of the Child Guidance Clinic in West Palm Beach were available for migrant children. When a child reacted abnormally or continued to be emotionally disturbed and maladjusted, he was referred to the clinic where he was tested by a psychologist and a program of treatment was outlined. However, it often was impossible for the school to follow through with the recommendations. Since continued treatment involved trips for both parents and children, it proved to be difficult and costly. Indeed, parents, in a number of cases, were reluctant even to make an initial trip with their children because they did not understand the need for care and because they could not afford the loss of working time. Nevertheless, the schools made full use of the services of the psychological worker on those days in which she was available in the Glades area.

Teachers themselves attempted to create an atmosphere in the classroom for good mental health. They recognized the problems and achievements of the children, encouraged those who had special talents, and made every effort to supply satisfactions in school which would overcome problems at home.

Although it was recognized that to accomplish all that was necessary to insure good mental health for every child was impossible, the results do indicate that children became better adjusted and happier while enrolled in school.

The practical arts

The practical arts—instruction in such skills as child care, preparation of food, making and alteration of clothing, home nursing, building and repair of furniture, and wood finishing—are an important part of the school program for migrants. Since these children carry family responsibilities at an early age, they need vocational training to meet problems of daily living. Since many drop out of school before reaching high school, this training is necessary in school as early as possible.

Although under the handicap of insufficient facilities and personnel, schools provided opportunities, within the regular classroom and school program or through club activities, for children to learn practical skills.

Though more extensive than in other schools, the program developed in one school located in a labor housing center, of which migrant children made up 60 percent of the annual enrollment, illustrates the work being done in the schools to meet the needs of these children.

During the first year of the Project, the faculty initiated an experimental program in homemaking. One of the tin shelters located near the school building was given rent-free by the director of the housing authority for making a shelter into a demonstration center of improved home living and for giving the children practical homemaking experience.

BOYS EQUIP SHELTER FOR USE

The first project was to prepare the shelter for use. Sixth-grade boys, under the direction of their teacher, cleaned and painted the building; repaired the back wall; installed a kitchen sink and running water, which was piped from the public water hydrant nearby; constructed work counters and cabinets; and installed a gas stove and electric refrigerator. The latter were furnished by the county board; the sink was donated by a local citizen. The boys planned and checked carefully to find the stores offering the best buys, accompanied their teacher to purchase materials and supplies, and kept a record of all expenses. The school spent less than $10 on the project.

Actual work time was scheduled for the last period of the school day, but since the boys lived in the camp, work frequently continued after the regular school hours. The project lasted through the school term. The next year, even though the boys did some additional work, the shelter was used primarily for cooking and serving meals. The sixth-grade girls, under the direction of the principal and the first-grade teacher, worked on sewing projects while the boys worked on the shelter.

OTHER WOODWORKING AND REPAIR PROJECTS

After the tin shelter was completed, the teachers continued to give direction to other practical construction projects for fifth- and sixth-grade boys. Under the supervision of the sixth-grade teacher, the boys designed and made bookshelves, tables, and desks, and built and painted a stage setting for the school's Thanksgiving and Christmas programs. Construction of library shelves provided an opportunity for the boys to learn to measure accurately and to compute the amount and cost of lumber.

In the meantime, the boys also assumed responsibility for doing simple repair jobs around the school. They divided into small committees, each group responsible for making its own plans and checking the necessary tools and materials. The repair of steps, desks, tables, broken window panes, door bolts, locks, window blinds, swings, seesaws, and other playground equipment was supervised by a teacher.

Interest continued in repair and maintenance work. The boys considered themselves a special group needed in the school. The principal reported that this kind of experience "gave the boys a feeling of importance, encouraged them to remain in school, and increased their interest in the academic subjects."

PLANNING, COOKING, AND SERVING MEALS

Fifth- and sixth-grade girls took part in a project for planning, cooking, and serving meals. The principal gave general supervision and one of the teachers frequently assisted them with special problems—the preparation of cream sauce and kneading dough—

but since most members of the faculty had teaching duties during the actual preparation of meals, their participation consisted mainly of helping during the planning and evaluation periods. Groups of four or five girls took turns planning, cooking, and serving. Each meal was evaluated in terms of preparation, nutrition, and cost.

The planning periods were learning experiences, and the girls found that they spent more time in planning and evaluating a meal than in actual preparation. Attention was given to the use of low-cost nutritious food, and records were kept on the cost of each meal. With the exception of staple groceries, most of the food served was either donated by packing houses or brought from home, each girl contributing a share.

Luncheon was served in the shelter. The girls took turns serving as hostess, and a guest was always invited. Usually, the guest was a migrant mother; occasionally, the home agent, representatives from the county health and education departments, teachers, and boys from their classes came. One luncheon menu included green bean chop suey, creamed potatoes, tossed green salad, Michigan cherries with tapioca cream, buttermilk biscuits, and iced tea. A mother of one of the girls sent the recipe for the chop suey. The green beans and the greens for the salad were donated by a packing house. The potatoes and canned cherries were brought from home by different girls. The guest was a migrant mother who had canned the cherries while living in Michigan during the past harvest season. Six people were served and the cost of the meal was one dollar.

Parents took a special interest in the project and helped by supplying fresh vegetables from the packing houses where they worked. Mothers came to see the kitchen or to show a neighbor "what the girls are doing." They spoke of the need for every girl to learn to cook well and talked about the nice kitchen and its conveniences.

SEWING PROJECTS

The sewing project, which included all the girls in the fifth and sixth grades and a few interested girls from the lower grades, was under the direction of the principal, 4-H Club leaders, and workers from the Christian Ministry. Usually, one of the primary teachers worked with the girls during the last period of the day, but much of the sewing was done after school hours. Parents donated two used sewing machines. Many of the materials—feed sacks, cotton remnants, patterns, and sewing kits—were supplied by local church groups, teachers, and people in the community. The project provided opportunities for the girls to learn to make and outfit sewing kits, operate a sewing machine, select material, fit patterns, and make, remodel, and repair clothing.

The project was integrated with the 4-H Club program and gave impetus to such 4-H projects as food preparation, child care, gardening, home improvement, and recreation. Prior to the county 4-H Achievement Day the school held a public program at which time all girls modeled the clothing they had made. Fifteen girls who had completed three or more 4-H projects were presented with 4-H Club pins. These girls also participated in the Achievement Day program. Later, eight of them made and modeled dresses at the annual dress revue sponsored by a community organization.

NURSERY- AND FLOWER-PLANTING PROJECT

A nursery- and flower-planting project was begun "to beautify the school grounds, to encourage the children to make their homes more attractive, to encourage the pursuit of a worthwhile hobby, and to develop . . . appreciation in natural science." Children in the fourth, fifth, and sixth grades participated. They placed soil in tin cans and planted small cuttings of flowers, shrubs, and bulbs. Some of the children brought cuttings and plants from their homes or from those of neighbors. A seed bed was made on the school grounds from which plants were either transplanted to containers for use in the classrooms or taken by the children to plant near their homes.

As the project developed and special attention to the care and protection of the plants transplanted on the school grounds was needed, the children of the lower grades joined in the work, making participation school-wide. Girls learned to make flower arrangements which were used in the classrooms and in the tin shelter when they served luncheons and were sent home when a child, or a member of his family, was ill or had a birthday.

The project gave students a sense of pride in their work and an appreciation for the beauty of plants and flowers. Several children went on to choose flower–planting projects for their 4-H Club work.

RESULTS

This program in the practical arts had favorable results for all the participants. Children developed proficiency in useful skills and a sense of belonging to the school. Teachers learned to use their special abilities and interests to strengthen the total school program. Parents became more interested in the work taking place in school. And the community became more sensitive to the type of contribution agencies and individuals could make to help the school.

Other schools adopted programs of vocational-type training in woodworking, home furnishing, meal-planning, and sewing. In one of the larger schools, a special home-nursing class for the girls of the seventh and eighth grades, most of whom were migrants, was organized and taught by the home economics teacher. Demonstrations were given in which the girls participated. They learned the correct method of making a bed for a sick person, of reading a thermometer, of giving a bed bath, of giving an enema, of preparing and using a bedpan, and of disinfecting a sick room. The teacher reported that the girls were very interested in the class, and out of the 38 originally enrolled, 32 received home-nursing certificates.

Extending educational opportunities

Work can be done to increase the number of migrant children enrolling in school. Parents can be convinced of the value of education. Communities can be made aware of their responsibility for the education of these children. Outside aid may be solicited for funds to employ additional personnel to accommodate larger numbers of migrants. But the schools alone cannot alter the migratory pattern of these people's lives. However, teachers can welcome and accept each migrant child as an important person who has a place in the school. They can teach so as to make each day most valuable for these children. In addition, teachers can initiate classroom activities and help children to develop individual plans which can be carried forward independently when they travel. While it is difficult to measure the tangible results of such work, the enthusiasm of the children while preparing on-the-trek projects and their usefulness in present learning indicate that the activities are valuable.

IDENTIFYING TRAVEL ROUTES

Contacts were made with crewleaders, foremen of traveling groups, and the local employment offices to identify prospective travel routes. Though patterns have innumerable variations, and it is impossible to identify accurately a route for any child, two patterns of travel were mapped and studied, the route from Florida to Michigan and the route along the eastern shore from Florida to New York via Virginia.

Migrant crewleaders and other foremen of traveling families and groups contributed information insofar as they knew their schedule plans. Several crewleaders indicated an interest in trying to arrange their travel schedule so that the children could visit some historical points of interest. One said, "You let us know where you

117

want us to stop, and we'll try to do that." Another, "We'd like to see some of these places ourselves."

Information was collected on places of interest—agricultural centers, parks, educational foundations, historical monuments, industries, zoos, and natural attractions—along the routes of the workers. From this information, a pictorial map was compiled of educational and historical sites so that the children could become familiar with the route they traveled.

To acquaint children with the work of their parents and to help them understand agricultural enterprises, teachers showed films and slides on the growth and harvesting of crops. They also made trips to vegetable fields, packing houses, and the Agricultural Experiment Station, and interviewed people taking part in local agricultural enterprises.

DEVELOPING MATERIAL FOR USE ON THE ROAD

The materials developed for migrants to take with them were included in notebooks, scrapbooks, and booklets.

Teachers helped children compile special notebooks with reading, spelling, language, and arithmetic activities to use while they traveled. Some exercises the children had already studied and were to review so that they would be sure to remember what they had learned. Others were independent activities to be completed as they traveled—words to remember, number and word games, lists of crops growing, and diaries.

Some children made individual scrapbooks with pictures, clippings, and illustrative materials of the school and community activities and of the places through which they would probably travel. Resident children contributed to these scrapbooks, and all children offered suggestions of what the migrant children could add to them as they traveled.

One first-grade teacher made booklets consisting of duplicated copies of supplementary stories taken from the teacher's guide used in the developmental reading program, and the children drew their own pictures to illustrate the stories. Upon withdrawal, the booklet was given to the child with a request to read it as he traveled, and to try to add his own stories and pictures of what he saw while traveling.

A third-grade teacher purchased individual experience tablets for the 30 migrant children in her class. "As we developed our experience stories daily, each child copied his story in his tablet," she reported, "and sometimes after we had a review lesson on the basic number concepts, I had them add these exercises since I felt that these were the kinds of things on which they needed much drill." The children were to take the tablets with them to read and study while they were gone. The teacher wrote a personal note for each child to his "new" teacher asking that she guide him in developing other stories so that he could have something additional to read and study. She believed that "since these children know that they will take the tablets with them, it causes them to do a better job of their writing and number work."

Teachers encouraged the children to write daily diaries while traveling and to list the places of interest they visited, the crops they saw, and any information about the areas in which they stopped or lived. One 12-year-old boy returned with the following diary, illustrative of the possibilities for learning from this activity:

Travel Diary of Mark Fields

Georgia
May 14, 1957

The climate is cool and rainy in Georgia. It has a lot of cows and hogs. The towns are not very big. Atlanta is a big town. We saw some army troops going on vanoovers [maneuvers]. Georgia has very many peach trees.

Tennessee
May 15, 1957

Tennessee has a warm climate. It has lots of ponies and horses. It has more pigs than any kind of animal. Nashville and Chattanooga have very high mountains. They are very big towns, too. In Chattanooga is Lookout Mountain and Ruby Falls.

Illinois
May 16, 1957

Illinois is a very big state. We traveled two days in it. It has very green valleys. East Dubuque, Ill., is not a big town. It has a warm and cold climate. Chicago is really a big city in Ill. It has a little bit of everything. The population of Chicago is 3,620,962. The state of Illinois is the land of Abraham Lincoln. In Galena, Illinois is where Ulysseess [Ulysses] S. Grant lived. In Chicago is a big statue of Lincoln.

Iowa
May 18, 1957

Across the bridge from Illinois is Iowa. It has about the same climate as Ill. Dubuque, Iowa is a pretty big town. It has plenty of Theatres. It has green valleys. In Marquette, Iowa there is the longest bridge across water that trains go across. It is called the Pontune [pontoon] bridge. It extends across the Mississippi River. Iowa is noted for its corn. They call it the corn state.

Summary and recommendations

This Project opened up promising approaches to the solution of many of the problems faced by migrant children and their families. Final evaluation of the Project should be made in terms of its contribution to the education of migrant children in Palm Beach County, Florida, and Northampton County, Virginia, and its contribution to other communities in their efforts to improve the lives of those who follow the crops.

Through the Project the two communities became more sensitive to the educational problems related to migrancy and to their responsibilities as communities whose economies depend upon a large migrant labor force. More specifically, their school boards, administrators, and teachers learned to solve educational problems more effectively: they refined promising administrative and instructional techniques in operation at the opening of the Project, tested and adopted new ones, and by the close of the Project were more competent in dealing with the professional challenges presented by migrant children.

The development of more effective programs to aid migrant families is essential to the solution of their problems. To be most effective and efficient in accomplishing results in the minimum period of time, such development must take place at the community, state, and national levels, and not only in education but in every social service affecting migrants. The basic approach to helping migrants, however, is through education. The conclusions and recommendations which follow are oriented to this approach.

As noted in the Foreword, in the preceding chapters, the writer has attempted to report objectively what has happened and what she has observed. Out of this experience she has developed some strong convictions, the most important of which are summarized in this chapter.

Palm Beach County, Florida, and Northampton County, Virginia, provided an ideal setting for a pilot project on the education of agricultural migratory children: (a) Many migrant children attended these schools, which represent both the home-base and on-the-trek situations; (b) several nationalities and ethnic groups were represented in both situations; (c) the two counties maintain progressive school systems which are concerned with the problems involved in the education of agricultural migratory children; (d) to a limited extent the two local areas served the same migratory children; and (e) these two areas carry on agricultural enterprises representing both large industrial managements and small type farms.

• There are many areas in the United States in which experimental programs could profitably be developed through the cooperation of two or more school systems.

LEARNING ABOUT MIGRANTS

Teachers are unaware of the life pattern of the migrant child, of the facts of life as he knows them, and of his deprivations. The nurture and protection that we hold to be the heritage of the child in his family within the community are far removed from the actualities of life as experienced by the migrant child. The concepts a migrant child forms about himself are reinforced not only by his own cultural group but through his contacts with nonmigrant cultural groups. These contacts create feelings of insecurity in him when he faces situations in his daily life.

Work must be done, then, by teachers and teacher-education institutions and through research to understand the migrant child and his needs.

• Each teacher should become acquainted with the actual facts in the life of the migrant children whom she teaches.

• If a migrant child is to become more nearly the kind of person he is capable of becoming, teachers must help him to acquire an adequate self-concept as he matures so that he will feel secure and be open to new experiences.

• Teacher-training institutions should provide preservice and inservice programs specially designed to give teachers basic concepts and understanding of (a) the cultural patterns to be found among migrants; (b) the essential elements inherent in the national phenomenon of agricultural migratory labor; (c) the agricultural economy of our nation; (d) the contributions to the local and national economy made by agricultural migratory workers;

and (e) the fundamentals of social anthropology, child growth and development, welfare, and health.

• Research should be conducted to investigate the developmental tasks which a migrant child is expected to accomplish in his own culture and the conflicts which develop during his school experience as a result of these expectations.

• Research should be conducted to identify the inhibiting self-concepts of migrant children and to determine the experiences which schools may offer to change these concepts.

ESTABLISHING FRIENDLY RELATIONS

A new school situation often is threatening to the migrant child. The most significant problem confronting teachers is how to help him feel that he is wanted, important, and adequate. Not until rapport is established between the teacher and the migrant child and he feels at home does learning take place. When teachers welcome the child warmly, help him to gain acceptance by his peers, and establish friendly relations among the school, the home, and the child, the migrant usually will assimilate his school experiences rapidly.

• Teachers should prepare resident children for the coming of migrant children by helping them to understand why these children move from place to place, and why their parents' work is important.

• Schools should welcome and accept each migrant child as an important person who has a place in the school.

• Teachers should make friendly contacts with the parents by visiting the homes and arrange for the parents to visit and participate in the school program.

ESTABLISHING PRIORITIES

Migrant children need the same proficiencies and skills as all American children. But, because their life pattern varies and their school experiences are irregular, there are some skills to which schools must give priority. The fundamental skills of literacy are so important that teachers receiving these children at any grade level should give them the basic reading competencies, fundamental number concepts, and speaking and writing proficiencies. Along with these fundamentals, migrant children need educational experiences which give them direction toward improving their lives.

The basic principles of teaching are the same for all children. But, if schools are to provide learning experiences which meet the special needs of migrant children and which compensate more nearly for their irregular school attendance, then all schools must make some modifications of instructional patterns, of curriculum content and materials, and of the development of specialized materials.

• Insofar as possible, migrant children should be placed in classrooms according to their chronological age, physical maturity, and social development regardless of their grade placement and academic achievement and instruction should be adapted to the children's individual attainment levels.

• Teachers should determine as quickly and accurately as possible the levels of performance of each migrant child in the basic skills—reading, writing, speaking, spelling, and arithmetic.

• Teachers should understand the unique experiences and distinctive needs of each migrant child and provide learning experiences which take into account his experiences and which meet his needs.

• Research should be conducted to develop and test feasible methods for determining the best classroom placement and the instructional levels of each migrant child.

• Studies should be conducted to identify the basic minimum competencies which migrant children need.

• Arrangements should be made whereby teacher-preparation institutions may provide special inservice programs for administrators, supervisors, classroom teachers, special teachers, and other professional personnel which are designed to deal specifically with the modifications of instructional patterns, methods, curriculum, and materials, and other problems involved in teaching migrant children.

• Schools should explore the possibilities of cooperative teaching for the purpose of serving their migrant children more effectively.

• Arrangements should be made for local school systems to explore further the services that can be available through the employment of additional helping teachers.

• Studies should be conducted to determine the difference in the kind and extent of learning when migrants are integrated in regular classrooms and when they are taught in classrooms where all children are migrants.

• Research should be conducted to determine the number of non-English-speaking children who can be taught effectively in integrated classrooms.

HELPING MIGRANT CHILDREN LEARN

Appropriate instructional materials for use by migrant children are limited. There is need for much easy reading material which is geared more nearly to the actual experiences and interests of these children. The usual textbooks often are frustrating to the migrant child. The vocabulary load is likely to be too heavy for him since his limited experiences do not afford him proper background to interpret meanings. The grammatical construction is different from his own language pattern and the content presented is outside the range of his life experiences. Unless teachers are alert to the difficulties which textbooks may present to the migrant child and make the necessary adaptations, his feelings of inadequacy will be reinforced and learning will be inhibited.

• Teachers should select instructional materials which relate more nearly to the interests, experiences, and needs of migrant children and which present a vocabulary comparable to their individual levels of reading performance.

• Teachers should develop teaching materials which are geared to the experiences, interests, and needs of the migrant children whom they teach.

• Studies should be conducted to develop and test the use of testing-teaching materials for migrant children, including Spanish-speaking children.

MEETING HEALTH NEEDS

Migrant children have varied health needs, many of which must be met immediately if the child is to attend school and be healthy enough to learn effectively. The schools must work cooperatively with health departments, local agencies and organizations, and parents.

• Schools should make use of available and appropriate health services and agencies to improve health conditions of migrants.

• Teachers should obtain professional advice and assistance in identifying special health needs of migrant children and in the adapting of health instruction to meet such needs.

GIVING MIGRANTS PRACTICAL TRAINING

Migrant children early in life need to develop proficiencies in practical skills. Since they carry family responsibilities at an early age, they need practical knowledge for immediate use in their daily lives. Schools can do much to prepare them more adequately for their home responsibilities and for their travel and work experiences, and can give them better understanding of the effective use of their money and of the means of earning a livelihood which are open to them.

• Elementary schools should provide experiences for migrant children so they can develop proficiencies in the practical arts and skills.

• Vocational-type training should be made available to migrant boys and girls at the junior high-school level.

LEARNING THROUGH TRAVEL

Though the travels of the migrant child offer many opportunities for meaningful learning experiences, he is not likely to be aware of the rich knowledge to be gained through his travels. When teachers ask about these unique experiences and take them into account in teaching him and when they develop projects and materials designed to guide and extend learning experiences while traveling, the child will become more aware of the educational values of his travel.   If he receives such guidance in every school, the knowledge acquired during his travels will compensate more nearly for the schooling he misses.

• Teachers should give the migrant child opportunity to draw upon his travel experiences to make contributions to classroom activities.

• Teachers should plan classroom projects and develop materials to help migrant children extend their educational experiences while traveling.

HELP FROM THE COMMUNITY

Schools serving migrant children must have the support of community agencies and organizations. Through cooperative arrangements with local agencies, organizations, and interested citizens much needed information and services can be extended to children and their families. Generally, the degree to which community agencies and organizations provide services to migrant families depends upon the extent of their understanding of the migrant situation and of the problems and needs of the children and their families. When schools assume the responsibility for contacting these groups and for interpreting to them the problems involved in the migrant situation and the needs of the children, they find many resources available to them, and support is given to programs designed to improve the welfare of these children. Furthermore, when cooperative effort is made by schools and community groups to improve the lives of migrant residents, the educational horizons of the community are raised and the general welfare of all residents is improved.

• Schools should identify, develop, and make use of the services of community agencies and organizations in the promotion of the education and general welfare of migrant children and their families.

STATE AND NATIONAL SUPPORT

Problems in the education of migrant children best can be resolved through programs of cooperative study and action on the local levels. However, local schools must have adequate support and technical professional assistance from the state departments of education, teacher-training institutions, the state education associations and the National Education Association, the United States Office of Education, and other appropriate local, state, and national agencies to carry on the type of inservice education programs needed.

• Local school systems which serve migrant children should employ additional supervisory personnel specifically assigned the responsibility of improving the learning situation of migrant children.

• State departments of education should sponsor arrangements whereby short work conferences for school personnel from adjacent counties may be held at regularly spaced intervals through the year to deal with the special problems involved in the education of migrant children.

• School systems, in cooperation with state departments of education and teacher-training institutions, should sponsor workshops, institutes, and extension courses for school personnel in local areas during the time migrant children are in residence.

• The United States Office of Education and the state departments of education (in those states in which migrants reside) should employ additional staff personnel to serve as specialists or consultants in the education of agricultural migratory children whose duties would include: (a) representing the interest of migrant children before local, state, and national professional organizations, agencies, and lay groups; (b) assisting in the development and conduct of inservice educational programs; (c) initiating and supervising special projects designed for the conduct of needed research; and (d) cumulating, analyzing, and disseminating information.

SCHOOL RECORDS AND REPORTS

Precise, accurate, and objective information on a specially designed report, or written as an informal note from the teacher, is of much value in the accurate and ready placement of the child in school. One of the most valuable sources of information to the receiving teacher is the directed self-evaluation made by the migrant child. Under the guidance of each teacher the migrant child may record regularly, with each entry dated, what he has learned to do, the subjects on which he needs to work, the books he has read, what he wants to learn, and the problems which are disturbing to him. This type of self-evaluation record kept by the child not only will be valuable as a school transfer record but will aid his own learning and development.

• Teachers should give each migrant child upon withdrawal a school report or an informal note containing accurate, precise, and objective information needed for the receiving teacher to readily place him for his best learning.

• Teachers should experiment with the development of self-evaluation records to be kept and carried by migrant children.

SCHOOL ENROLLMENT AND ATTENDANCE

Nonenrollment in school and irregular school attendance patterns of migrant children are caused by: (a) the problems inherent in migrancy itself; (b) the failure of migrant parents to realize the value of an education; (c) the unawareness of some communities that migrant children reside in their areas and of their responsibility for the education of these children; (d) the excessive cost of the provision for school facilities and teaching personnel needed to accommodate large numbers of migrant children; and (e) an administrative pattern that closes the schools during the height of the cropping season.

• Teachers should encourage migrant children to enroll in school in every community in which they reside and make contacts repeatedly with parents and crewleaders for the same purpose.

• Visiting teachers—professionally trained personnel who serve as a liaison between the school and the home and who work to relieve conditions which prevent children from attending school regularly—should be employed in areas where migrant children reside, even for brief periods during a year.

• Local school systems should include the listing of migrant children in their regular school census.

• The identity and count of migrant adults and children should be included in the decennial United States Census.

• Each community should arrange for its school to be in session while the migrant labor force is present.

• The United States Office of Education should cumulate and analyze information on the enrollment and attendance of agricultural migratory children to identify the areas in which adequate schooling is, and is not, provided.

• The appropriate personnel of state departments of education should make thorough investigation and analysis of the current procedures of allocating monies to local school systems in order that the systems may derive more equitable formulas for the financial support of areas serving large numbers of agricultural children.

• The federal and state governments should enact legislation for the appropriation of monies to subsidize local school systems that serve large numbers of migrant children.

APPENDIX I

Project Sponsors

The National Council on Agricultural Life and Labor is a coordinating council for agencies sharing its defined purposes: ". . . to improve the living and working conditions of the low income farm and rural populations of the United States of America by all possible means, including the collection and dissemination to organizations and individuals of information of scientific, economic, social, literary, and educational character."

The seven cosponsoring agencies of the original research project were: (a) American Friends Service Committee, (b) Council for Social Action, Congregational Christian Churches, (c) Department of Rural Education, National Education Association, (d) Division of Home Missions, National Council of Churches of Christ in the United States of America, (e) National Catholic Rural Life Conference, (f) National Child Labor Committee, and (g) the National Council on Agricultural Life and Labor.

For purposes of this Pilot Project the Migrant Research Project Board was enlarged by the addition of representatives of the Alliance for the Guidance of Rural Youth and the National Sharecroppers Fund, and by a consultant from the United States Office of Education. Later the Migrant Research Project Board became the Migrant Research Fund of the NCALL.

APPENDIX II

Advisory Committees

After the initial months of the Project, it seemed evident that school advisory committees were needed to give directions to the program in each county. The superintendent in each situation made the official appointments. In Palm Beach County there were two committees—one for the Negro schools and one for the white—which were composed of the principals and teachers representative of the various levels of teaching. In Northampton County there was only one committee since all but a negligible few were Negro children. This committee was composed of the principals and a classroom teacher from each school, the superintendent, and the two supervisors—Negro and white. As the Project developed, additional teachers were added to each of these in order to give wider representation. The committees were known as the Advisory Committees on the Education of Migratory Children. The Supervisor gave continuing leadership to each committee, while the other instructional supervisors served as ex-officio members in Palm Beach County.

131

Northampton County, Virginia

W. F. Lawson, Jr., Division Superintendent
B. Gordon Wescott, Elementary Supervisor of White Schools
Cora Campbell, Elementary Supervisor of Negro Schools

Cape Charles Elementary School
Jesse L. Hare, teacher.

Capeville School
Clarence Arnold, principal; George T. Allen, Mrs. Zelma L. Bragg, Mrs. Delcia
Bell Staten, teachers; Mrs. Marie S. Griffin, helping teacher.

Hare Valley
Johnny Worsley, principal; Homer Q. Collins, Mrs. Madge S. Green, Mrs.
Margaret U. Rayfield, Mrs. Mary S. Rogers, Mrs. Emma Geskins Spady, Mrs.
Marguerite D. Spady, Mrs. Pauline W. Spady, teachers; Mrs. Eloise Spady
Baylark,* Mrs. Ida S. Collins, Mrs. Thessa B. Downing,* helping teachers.

Machipongo
Otis Bragg, principal; Mrs. Alice B. Brown, Mrs. Jeanette McC. Monroe, Mrs.
Daisy O. Poole, Mrs. Lency D. Treherne, teachers; Frances P. Bibbins,*
Miss Lois A. Downing,* helping teachers.

Northampton County High School
W. H. Smith, principal; Doris M. Turner, librarian.

Palm Beach County, Florida

Howell L. Watkins, Superintendent of Instruction
Mrs. Clara Hunter Capron, Director of Instruction

Belle Glade School
Frank O. Hobson, principal; Mrs. Margaret Mosley, assistant principal; Mrs.
Ann K. Lovell, elementary teacher; Wayne Fortenberry, Kathleen Rogers,
high-school teachers; Mrs. Nancy W. Boots, special services.

Bryant School
Mrs. Elexina E. Davis, principal.

Canal Point Camp School
Mrs. Christine B. Jackson, principal.

Canal Point School
Carl Crawford, principal.

East Lake Junior High School
Stanleigh M. Murrell, principal; Willie Walker, elementary teacher; Mrs
Lillie W. Reed, teacher.

---

*Miss Bibbins and Mrs. Downing served as helping teachers during the
first year of the Program, and upon resignation were replaced the second year
by Miss Downing and Mrs. Baylark.

Everglades Camp School
Arthur King, principal; Mrs. Myrtis Burke, teacher.

Lake Harbor School
Lloyd L. Williams, principal.

Lake Shore School
Charles M. McCurdy, principal; Eddie H. Fitzgerald, assistant principal; Marion M. Hamilton, assistant principal and dean of boys; Mrs. Muriel J. Evans, teacher; Mrs. Ernestine B. Moore, home economics teacher.

Okeechobee School
Elmo St. Greaux, principal; Mrs. Shirley D. Weaver, elementary teacher; Mrs. Elizabeth Powell, teacher; Mrs. Theola H. Reddick, special education services.

Osceola School
Mrs. Ruth S. Irvin, principal; Mrs. Mabel R. Lutz, Mrs. Dorothy McDonald, elementary teachers.

Pahokee School
Clyde Canipe, principal; Brooks Henderson, assistant principal; Mrs. Kathryn Cunningham, Mrs. Fern Frank, elementary teachers; Mrs. Doris Lane, home economics teacher; Mrs. Evelyn Lair, special services.

Rosenwald School
Getchrell Singleton, principal; Mrs. Evelyn P. Mitchell, teacher.

South Bay School
Pellon Morris, principal; Mrs. Edrie Maxwell, elementary teacher.

Attendance Workers

Mrs. Lily Register; Samuel L. Teague, Sr.

Music Coordinators

Cora Lee Scott; Mrs. Ruth Snyder.

Ex-Officio Members

Hazel St. Clair,* Supervisor of Negro Schools, Palm Beach County.
Britton G. Sayles, principal, Roosevelt High School, West Palm Beach, served as an informal consultant to this group from time to time.

In addition to the superintendent and director of instruction the following members of the county's supervisory staff served ex officio and met with both advisory committees from time to time:
Mrs. Marjorie Crick, Coordinator of Program for Exceptional Children
Mrs. Jane Lansing, Supervisor of School Lunch Program
Mrs. Ivyl Pirtle, Supervisor of Elementary Education
Mrs. Olean Strayhorn, Supervisor of Secondary Education.

---

*Deceased

APPENDIX III

Special Bilingual Language Materials for Spanish-Speaking Children

Though English was used at all times for instruction, special materials were developed to help the Spanish-speaking children learn to speak and read the English language.

Classroom Objects Labeled

Teachers found that the labeling of classroom objects helped the child to develop a vocabulary, and prompted him to make inquiries about the school environment and activities. A tagboard strip, on which the name of the object was printed in English on one side and in Spanish on the reverse side, was fastened to the object. These labels were attached to all objects in the classroom. Frequently sentences such as, "This is a blackboard"; "Here are our pencils"; "This is Maria's chair"; "See the pretty flower"; and "Edmundo brought this rock to school" were also posted. These words and sentences were used in conversational periods, in games, for independent study, in the dictation and writing of stories, and in other ways.

Use of Pictures

Pictures that were simple in detail, colorful, clear, and of interest to children were collected and used. The child was asked to identify and to give the Spanish name of an object, and then to give the English equivalent. A sentence was written about the picture and attached to it. These words and sentences were transferred to strips of tagboard and used for matching words and sentences with appropriate objects and pictures. As the child's English vocabulary increased, with the help of his teacher, he dictated stories about his favorite pictures. These stories were transferred to reading charts and were accessible to the child for rereading, and for group reading with other children.

Translation of Picture Dictionary

Teachers found the translation and use of a picture dictionary to be useful in teaching Spanish-speaking children.[1] As the teacher and child examined the book together, the teacher printed the Spanish equivalent of each word and labeled the object pictured. One teacher wrote:

. . . Another outcome of this project was the warmth the child felt toward this book. In it, either through his own or through his parents' efforts, were words of his own tongue. In it were pictures he recognized. And

[1] Reed, Mary, and Osswald, Edith. *My Little Golden Dictionary.* New York: Simon & Schuster, 1949.

there, in large print, were the English words which he was so eager to learn. It became a book to keep close, to pore over. It led the child to want and to seek help from English-speaking classmates who could easily pronounce these strange, valuable words.

Scrapbooks of common pictures and objects were compiled to familiarize the child from another culture with his immediate surroundings and to increase his vocabulary. Several pages each were devoted to parts of the body, to family groups, to clothing, to pets, to household furnishings, to school experiences, to toys, and to agriculture. The page next to each group of pictures was left blank for appropriate words and sentences to be supplied by the child under the guidance of the teacher. Other pages were left unused so that additional material could be added as the scope of his learning widened.

Translation of Spanish Readers

For the Spanish-speaking child who was able to read his own language, but unable to read or speak English, teachers used a book translation from Spanish to English.[2] The English translation, made as literally as possible, was written in manuscript on the bottom of each page of the Spanish reader with the corresponding illustration sketched in pencil at the top. The child read the original and the translation. As he completed a page he was allowed to color the illustration. Teachers reported, "Again the visual correlation and comprehension of the new language with the known one were involved. . . . The reading resulting was not just recall of memorized vocabulary; it was meaningful expression in the second language."

Word Lists

The Dolch List of 220 Basic Words was translated into Spanish. Words were placed on strips of oak tag with a word printed in English on one side and in Spanish on the reverse side.[3] A list also was compiled containing the most essential words for communication at school and in the community. These words also were translated into Spanish.

Commonly Used Greetings and Expressions

In order to welcome the Spanish-speaking newcomer and to help him to become adjusted to his new school situation, teachers learned common expressions in Spanish. Effort was made to construct these questions and directions in English so that the Spanish translation would be similar to the way the Spanish child expresses himself:

Buenos días. (Good morning.)
Gracias. (Thank you.)
Me alegra que Ud. venga a la escuela. (I am happy that you are coming to school.)

---

[2] Hale, Lois, and Rhodes, Rueby S. *Juan y Maria* and *Juan y Maria en Casa.* The Amigos Panamericanos Series. Austin, Texas: The Steck Company.

[3] The Dolch List is not included here since it may be located in any professional library for teachers, and the 220 Basic Flash Cards—in both English and Spanish—may be purchased.

¿Dónde vive Ud.? (Where do you live?)
¿Dónde vivía Ud. antes de venir a aquí? (Where did you live before you came here?)
¿Iba Ud. a la escuela allí? (Did you go to school there?)
¿En que grado estaba Ud.? (What grade were you in?)
¿Cómo se llama Ud.? (What is your name?)
¿Cuántos años tiene Ud.? (How old are you?)
¿Cuántos hay en su familia? (How many are in your family?)
¿Cuántos hermanos tiene Ud.? (How many brothers do you have?)
¿Cuántos hermanas tiene Ud.? (How many sisters do you have?)
¿Van a la escuela? (Do they go to school?)
Ésta es su silla. (This is your seat [or] this is your chair.)
Éste es el lugar para su sobretodo. (Here is the place for your coat.)
¿Tiene Ud. papel? (Do you have paper?)
¿Tiene Ud. tigeras . . . lápiz . . . lápiz de color? (Do you have scissors . . . pencil . . . crayons?)
¿Va a almorzar en la escuela? (Are you going to eat lunch at school?)
¿Tiene Ud. dinero para su comida? (Do you have your lunch money?)
Estas niñas le van a ayudar. (These girls will help you.)
Estos niños le van a enceñar. (These boys will show you.)
Pare, por favor. (Stop, please.)
Póngase de pié, por favor. (Stand up, please [speaking to one child].)
Pónganse de pié, por favor. (Stand up, please [speaking to all children].)
Venga aquí, por favor. (Come here, please.)
¿Terminó Ud. su taréa? (or) trabajo? (Did you finish your task? [or] job? work?)
Contemos. (Let's count.)
Vamos a contar. (We are going to count.)
Uno, dos, tres, cuatro, cinco, seis, siete, ocho, nueve, deis. (One, two, three, four, five, six, seven, eight, nine, ten.)
Es hora de leer. (It is time to read.)
Es hora de escriber. (It is time to write.)
¿Como se dice esto en inglés? (How do you say this in English [teacher points to word or sentence]?)
¿Entiende (or) comprende Ud.? (Do you understand?)
Tráigame su papel (or) libro, por favor. (Bring me your paper . . . or book, please.)
Abra su libro, por favor. (Open your book, please.)
Lea esta historia . . . lección . . . página, por favor. (Read this story . . . lesson . . . page, please.)
Siéntese aquí, por favor. (Sit here, please.)
Siéntese, por favor. (Sit down, please.)
Póngalo (or) póngala aquí, por favor. (Put it here, please.)
No corra, por favor. (Do not run, please.)
Mine. (Look.)
Escuche. (Listen.)
De Ud. esta carta a su mamá, por favor. (Give this letter to your mother, please.)
Vaya a tomar agua. (Go get a drink.)
Puede ir al inodoro. (You may go to the bathroom.)
Puede irse. (You may go.)
Adios (or) hasta mañana. (Good-bye [or] see you tomorrow.)
Deseamos que haya estado contenta en la escuela, hoy. (We hope you have enjoyed our school today.)

SELECTED REFERENCES

A. General Background Information

A Desk for Billie. 57 min., 16mm, sound, color and b & w. National Education Association, Division of Press and Radio Relations, 1201 Sixteenth Street, N. W., Washington, D. C., 1960.
A film on the problems encountered in the education of migrant children.

Again . . . Pioneers. 68 min., 16mm, b & w, sound. Religious Film Associations, 35 W. 45th Street, New York, 1950.
A film on the attitude of communities toward migrant families.

ANDREWS, DOROTHEA. "Moppets Who Migrate." *Children* 1:85-91; May-June 1954.
An article on the complex social and economic problems of migrants in Florida and the attempts made by state and local authorities to cope with the situation.

BUREAU OF LABOR STANDARDS. *Selected References on Domestic Migratory Agricultural Workers and Their Families.* Washington, D. C.: U.S. Department of Labor. (In press)

Colorado Cares. 20 min., 16mm, sound, color. State Department of Health, Denver, Colorado, 1958.
How Mesa County initiated and expanded services to migrants through the formation of a county Migrant Council which brought together individuals and organizations concerned with the health, education, and general welfare of these people.

DAVIS, BILLIE. "And Here Is Your Desk . . . ." *NEA Journal* 45:337-38; September 1956.
The school desk is the symbol of this migrant child's "chance to participate in the world of real people."

EDWARDS, ESTHER P. "The Children of Migratory Agricultural Workers in the Public Elementary Schools of the United States: Needs and Proposals in the Area of Curriculum." *Harvard Educational Review* 30:12-52; Winter 1960.
A comprehensive review of the problems in education of migrant children and the attempts made to meet them.

FEDERAL INTERDEPARTMENTAL COMMITTEE ON CHILDREN AND YOUTH. *When the Migrant Families Come Again.* Washington, D. C.: Superintendent of Documents, Government Printing Office, 1955. 28 p.
Accounts of programs developed by communities.

137

FLORIDA STATE BOARD OF HEALTH, JACKSONVILLE. "Migrants Are People."
    Florida Health Notes 47:4; April 1955.
Study of the migrant situation in Florida, with special attention to health
problems and needs.

FULLER, VARDEN. *No Work Today! The Plight of America's Migrant.*
    Public Affairs Pamphlet No. 190. New York: Public Affairs Com-
    mittee (22 East 38th Street), 1953.

GOVERNOR'S STUDY COMMISSION ON MIGRATORY LABOR and THE INTER-
    AGENCY COMMITTEE ON MIGRATORY LABOR. *Migrants in Michigan.*
    Detroit: Division of Employment Security of the Michigan Employ-
    ment Security Commission (7310 Woodward Avenue), September
    1954. 36 p.
A handbook on migratory, seasonal, agricultural workers in Michigan, with
sections on educational programs for children and adults.

HERRING, ELIZABETH B., compiler. *A Partial Inventory of Programs with
    Children of Migratory Agricultural Workers.* Washington, D. C.
    National Council on Agricultural Life and Labor (1751 N Street,
    N.W.), September 15, 1958. (Mimeographed)
Summary of current programs for migrant children as sponsored by 18
national voluntary organizations and governmental agencies.

HURD, MERRILL F. *The Education of the Children of Agricultural Mi-
    grants in the Public Schools of New York State.* Doctor's thesis.
    New York: Syracuse University, 1960. 364 p.
A detailed investigation of the services available to the children of agricultural
migratory workers who come to New York State annually.

KOOS, EARL. *They Follow the Sun.* Jacksonville: Bureau of Maternal and
    Child Health, Florida Board of Health, 1957. 55 p.
Report of a project designed to identify the migrant's problems in his day-by-
day existence, and to give "reasonable explanations of why the migrant reacts
as he does to such services as are offered."

LEONE, LUCILE PETRY, and JOHNSTON, HELEN L. "Agricultural Migrants
    and Public Health." *Public Health Reports* 1:1-8; January 1954.
A general survey of the current situation of migrancy, including data concerning the living and working conditions, health situation and services,
and reviews and recommendations by different groups.

METZLER, WILLIAM H. *Migratory Farm Workers in the Atlantic Coast
    Stream.* Circular No. 966, U. S. Department of Agriculture. Wash-
    ington, D. C.: Superintendent of Documents, Government Printing
    Office, January 1955. 79 p.
Report of a field study of the employment and systematized movement of
migratory Negro workers in the Atlantic coast stream.

NATIONAL CONSUMERS COMMITTEE FOR RESEARCH AND EDUCATION, INC.
    Home Is Where They Find It. Cleveland, Ohio: the Committee

(348 Engineers Building), February 1958.

Description of a demonstration project among families of migrant agricultural workers in Marquette County, Wisconsin, in 1957.

PRESIDENT'S COMMITTEE ON MIGRATORY LABOR. *Migratory Labor in American Agriculture.* Washington, D. C.: Superintendent of Documents, Government Printing Office, 1951. 188 p.

A comprehensive report dealing with the social, economic, health, and educational conditions among migratory agricultural workers in the United States. Chapter 11, "Education," is of particular interest to teachers.

PRESIDENT'S COMMITTEE ON MIGRATORY LABOR. *Report to the President on Domestic Migratory Labor.* Washington, D. C.: Superintendent of Documents, Government Printing Office, September 1956. 36 p.

Reports of the Committee's organization activities and recommendations, including outlines of suggested regulations for labor camps and for the transportation of agricultural workers.

SUTTON, ELIZABETH. "The World of the Migrant Child." *Educational Leadership* 14:221-28; January 1957.

Discussion of the unique experiences and needs of migrant children, with emphasis on implications for schools and teacher-training institutions.

B. The Impact of the Rural Environment on Children

BATHURST, EFFIE G. *How Children Use the Community for Learning.* U.S. Department of Health, Education, and Welfare, Office of Education, Bulletin No. 6. Washington, D. C.: Superintendent of Documents, Government Printing Office, 1953. 46 p.

BATHURST, EFFIE G. *Where Children Live Affects Curriculum.* U.S. Department of Health, Education, and Welfare, Office of Education, Bulletin No. 7. Washington, D. C.: Superintendent of Documents, Government Printing Office, 1950. 77 p.

How groups of children and their teachers tackled everyday problems.

BATHURST, EFFIE G., and FRANSETH, JANE. *Modern Ways in One- and Two-Teacher Schools.* U.S. Department of Health, Education, and Welfare, Office of Education, Bulletin No. 18. Washington, D. C.: Superintendent of Documents, Government Printing Office, 1951. 48 p.

A discussion of practices that are helping rural boys and girls get a good education.

BUTTERWORTH, JULIAN E., and DAWSON, HOWARD A. *The Modern Rural School.* New York: McGraw-Hill, 1952. 494 p.

Community Resources in Teaching. 20 min., 16mm, sound, b & w. Iowa State University Bureau of Audio-Visual Instruction, Iowa City, 1950.

How a school made use of the community and its resources to adapt an educational program for children and adults.

DUNN, FANNIE W. *The Child in the Rural Environment.* 1951 Yearbook, Department of Rural Education, National Education Association. Washington, D. C.: the Association, 1951. 253 p. (Out of print)

A basic study of how the rural environment affects children's development.

HOPPOCK, ANNE, and OTHERS. *All Children Have Gifts.* Washington, D. C.: Association for Childhood Education International, 1958. 36 p.

Expresses the viewpoint that it is important to recognize and develop the giftedness in all children rather than to set apart the "gifted" few for special handling and assume that the others are adequately served by a more limited type of instruction.

OLSON, CLARA M., and FLETCHER, NORMAN D. *Learn and Live.* New York: Alfred P. Sloan Foundation (30 Rockfeller Plaza), 1946. 101 p.

A report of the Sloan Experiment in Applied Economics, concerned with the development of educational materials and practices which would meet food, housing, and clothing needs in rural areas.

PHI DELTA KAPPAN. "Current Problems in Rural Education." *Phi Delta Kappan* 36:1-67; October 1954.

The issue is devoted to problems of rural education. Articles by Lois M. Clark and Anne Hoppock deal with problems of classroom organization and the impact of the rural environment on children's learning.

School in Centreville. 20 min., 16mm, color and b & w. National Education Association, 1201 Sixteenth Street, N.W., Washington, D. C., 1950.

How pupils of one elementary school worked on community problems.

SOUTHERN STATES WORK CONFERENCE. *Rural Education in the South.* Tallahassee, Florida: State Department of Education, 1957.

A report of the conference on educational problems, 1954-57. Reviews the status of rural education in the South, with special emphasis on changes and trends. A list of recommendations for educational programs is included.

C. Accounts of Classroom Teaching and School Programs

ALLESSANDRO, JOSEPH. *School for Migrant Children.* University Park, Pennsylvania: College of Education, Pennsylvania State University, 1955. (Mimeographed)

Report of demonstration summer school held in Potter County, Pennsylvania: a total picture of the school—organization, curriculum, materials, testing program—and the individual progress made by the children.

ALWAY, LAZELLE D. *Will You Make a School?* Publication No. 421.

New York: National Child Labor Committee (419 Fourth Avenue), May 1957.
Brief descriptions of 13 experimental educational projects for migrant children which are representative of the programs attempted throughout the United States.

BAY COUNTY BOARD OF EDUCATION. *Bay County School for Migrant Children: July 3 through July 5, 1957.* Bay City, Michigan: Board of Education, 1957. (Mimeographed)
Brief report of a follow-up program initiated during the summer of 1956. Family case histories and program conclusions are of particular interest.

BLACKWOOD, PAUL E. "Migrants in Our Schools." *Educational Leadership* 14:207-13; January 1957.
Facts concerning the mobile population in the United States and implications for schools that focus attention on the special problems related to the education of migrant children.

COUGLIN, M. L. "So You Have Some Migrants in Your Classroom, Too?" *California Journal of Elementary Education* 18:57-64; August 1949.
Specific suggestions on ways of accepting and teaching the Spanish-speaking migrant child in the classroom.

DAVIS, BILLIE. "Life That Is Better Than Beans." *National Parent Teacher* 50:4-7; October 1955.
Story of the desire of one migrant child to be "somebody," and of how the free American schools helped her to fulfill this desire.

DIVISION OF HOME MISSIONS. *An Experiment in Vocational Education for the Children of Migratory Farm Workers, July-August 1956.* New York: National Council of the Churches of Christ in the U.S.A. (257 Fourth Avenue), 1956.
Report of a project conducted in a camp designed to give migrant boys and girls experiences which help to develop vocational skills. Adaptable to classroom use.

FLORIDA AGRICULTURAL AND MECHANICAL UNIVERSITY. *A Guide to the Education of Agricultural Migratory Children.* Tallahassee: the University (Edwin F. Norwood, Director of Extension Services), 1956. (Mimeographed)
Report of the extension class held in Palm Beach County, Florida, November 1955—March 1956, by the School of Education. Discussion of the needs of migrant children, with specific suggestions for meeting these needs in classrooms which enroll both resident and nonresident pupils.

FRESNO COUNTY SCHOOLS. *Home and Shop Arts.* Fresno, California: Office of County School Superintendent, 1954. (Mimeographed)
A teacher's notebook, for the experimental development of a program for schools in migrant areas, containing outline units in homemaking and industrial arts geared specifically to provide practical living experiences for

young people who will establish homes and become wage earners at an early age.

FRESNO COUNTY SCHOOLS. *Planning for the Child Who Moves.* The Educational Program for Migrant Children. Fresno, California: Office of County School Superintendent, 1954. (Mimeographed)

A tentative bulletin designed to experiment with better ways of working with migrant children. Includes specific suggestions and materials for the orientation of migrant children, as well as ways of adjusting the school program to meet the children's needs.

FRESNO COUNTY SCHOOLS. *Teaching Bilingual Children.* Fresno., California: Office of County School Superintendent, 1954. (Mimeographed)

A handbook of suggestions for teaching Spanish-speaking migrant children, with special attention to three types of learning experiences: informal learning through mixed work and play groups, periods for direct instruction, and special emphasis on the needs of these children in planning the regular classroom program.

FRESNO COUNTY SCHOOLS. *Teaching Children Who Move with the Crops.* Report and Recommendations of the Fresno County Project, The Educational Program for Migrant Children. (Prepared by Helen Cowan Wood.) Fresno, California: Office of County School Superintendent, 1955.

Directed to teachers who have migratory children enrolled in their classrooms. The book includes suggestions for working with the children.

GREENE, SHIRLEY E. *The Education of Migrant Children.* Washington, D. C.: Department of Rural Education, National Education Association, 1954. 179 p.

A comprehensive report of a field survey in counties in Florida, Virginia, Texas, and Illinois designed to determine the educational needs of migrant children.

HARDING, BILL. "Migrant Pupils: Challenge to Texas Education." *The Texas Outlook* 39:6-13; July 1955.

A comprehensive report on the problem of providing education for the 30,000 or more migratory children in Texas, and an explanation of the state's plan for financial assistance to school districts experiencing fluctuating scholastic enrollments.

JACKSON, DOROTHY S. "The Rootless Ones." *Delta Kappa Gamma Bulletin* 21:35-39; Winter 1955.

An account of New Jersey's summer school programs for migrant children.

LATTING, LUCILE H., editor. *Migrant Bilingual Workshop.* Denver: Office of Instructional Service, Colorado State Department of Education, 1957. (Mimeographed)

Report of a work conference for teachers held at Adams State College in Alamosa, Colorado, July 1957, with information on the cultural differences of Spanish-speaking migrants of the Southwest and the economic status of Spanish-speaking peoples in the United States.

LATTING, LUCILE H. *Reports of Colorado Summer Schools for Migrant Children, 1956-58.* Denver: Office of Instructional Services, Colorado State Department of Education. (Mimeographed)
A series of reports and daily diaries recorded by the teachers of the special summer schools held at Fort Lumpton, Palisade, Rocky Ford, and Wiggins.

MCCLURE, MORRIS. "Make Room for the Migrants." *Michigan Education Journal* 30:428-31; April 1953.
Presents the needs of migrant children and suggests that these needs can be met best when migrant children are accepted as "normal, educable children" in classrooms with resident children.

MANN, FRANK A. *Who Will Be Responsible?* University Park, Pennsylvania: College of Education, State University, 1957.
Report on the Pennsylvania State University school for migrant children, July-August 1957.

MARTIN, MARY MCCULLOM. "Story of Toltec School." *School Life* 37: 109-11; April 1955.
How one teacher helps migrant children in a school in Eloy, Arizona, in spite of many difficulties.

MORRISON, J. CAYCE. *A Letter to Friends of Puerto Rican Children.* The Puerto Rican Study. New York: Board of Education, 1955.
Nine propositions which teachers will find related to the problems of teaching migrant children.

NATIONAL EDUCATION ASSOCIATION, DEPARTMENT OF RURAL EDUCATION. *Helping Alvin Stay in School.* Rural Service Teaching Brief. Series 1, No. 1. Washington, D. C.: the Department, n.d.
How one teacher helped a boy to make the most of his potentialities through providing experiences at which he could succeed.

NATIONAL EDUCATION ASSOCIATION, DEPARTMENT OF RURAL EDUCATION. *Organizing the School To Help Children Learn To Read Better.* Rural Service Teaching Brief, Series 2, No. 1. Washington, D. C.: the Department, n.d.
How a teacher organized flexible groups to take care of the wide range of attainment levels and interests in reading among children, and helped them to improve their reading proficiency.

NEW JERSEY BUREAU OF MIGRANT LABOR. *Demonstration Schools for Migrant Children.* In annual reports of the Bureau of Migrant Labor, 1947-1960. Trenton: Department of Labor and Industry.
Reports of New Jersey's summer schools for migrant children, with emphasis on adapting teaching methods and curriculum to meet the children's needs.

NORTHAMPTON COUNTY SCHOOLS. *A Guide for the Teaching of Reading.* Eastville, Virginia: Northampton County School Board, 1956. (Mimeographed)
A report of the helping teacher program developed by the Pilot Project on the education of migratory children.

PALM BEACH COUNTY. *Hagen Road School, Delray Beach, Florida.* West
    Palm Beach, Florida: Director of Instruction, Palm Beach County
    Board of Public Instruction, 1958. (Mimeographed)
A report of a special school for Spanish-speaking migrant children, 1957-58.

NEW YORK CITY PUBLIC SCHOOLS. *Resource Units for Classes with
    Puerto Rican Pupils in the Fourth Grade, Experimental Edition.* Re-
    source Unit Series, The Puerto Rican Study. New York: Board of
    Education, November 1955.
Purposes, basic experiences, and related activities for three resource units.

NEW YORK CITY PUBLIC SCHOOLS. *A Guide to the Teaching of English to
    Puerto Rican Pupils—Intermediate Grades, Experimental Edition.*
    Language Guide Series, The Puerto Rican Study. New York: Board
    of Education, February 1956.
Suggestions and materials for use in teaching non-English-speaking children.
Teachers of Spanish-speaking migrant children will find this guide very
helpful.

PONITZ, H. J. "These, Too, Are Our Children." *Michigan Education
    Journal* 33:192-94; December 1955.
Report of the findings of a study made in Bay and Van Buren counties to
determine the number of migrant children in Michigan, the months they were
present, and their educational background.

RIVERSIDE PUBLIC SCHOOLS. *Practicum for Non-English-Speaking
    Children.* Developed by the Riverside Elementary School Faculty,
    1957-58. Miami, Florida: Dade County Board of Public Instruction.
    (Mimeographed)
Practical suggestions to teachers working with non-English-speaking children.

SCHOOL OF EDUCATION, FLORIDA STATE UNIVERSITY. *Working with
    Migrant Children in Our Schools.* Tallahassee: the University, 1956.
    (Mimeographed)
A handbook for teachers engaged in teaching children enrolled in schools
serving both resident and migrant populations as developed by the extension class at Palm Beach County, Florida, November 1955-April 1956.

SHERMAN, NEIL W., editor. *Nomads of the Classroom.* Tempe, Arizona:
    College of Education, Arizona State College, January 1958.
    (Mimeographed)
Report of a five-week workshop on the education of migrant children held at
Arizona State College.

SUTTON, ELIZABETH. "Welcome to Our School, Jim." *NEA Journal* 46:
    42-3; January 1957.
How some schools help migrant children to become oriented, and how teachers
use the children's unique travel and work experiences in teaching them.

U.S. DEPARTMENT OF HEALTH, EDUCATION, AND WELFARE, OFFICE OF EDUCATION. *Report of the East Coast Migrant Conference.* Washington, D. C.: Superintendent of Documents, Government Printing Office, 1954. (Duplicated)
The migrant situation and the efforts of national and state organizations— both public and voluntary—interested in the health, education, and welfare problems of migrants in 10 Coast states.

U.S. DEPARTMENT OF HEALTH, EDUCATION, AND WELFARE, OFFICE OF EDUCATION. *Report of Regional Conferences on Education of Migrant Children.* Washington, D. C.: Superintendent of Documents, Government Printing Office, 1952. (Mimeographed)
Digest of four regional conferences concerned with problems of schooling for migrant children.

U.S. DEPARTMENT OF HEALTH, EDUCATION, AND WELFARE, OFFICE OF EDUCATION. *Report of Two Conferences on Planning Education for Agricultural Migrants.* Prepared by Paul E. Blackwood. Washington, D. C.: Superintendent of Documents, Government Printing Office, July 1957. 58 p. (Duplicated)
Summary of programs to improve the education of migrants, with a discussion of local, state, and regional problems and recommendations for solving them.

WEBER, JULIA. *My Country Diary.* New York: Harper and Brothers, 1946. 270 p.
The experiences of a creative teacher in working with the children and families in a somewhat isolated community.

WOOD, HELEN COWAN. "Children Who Move with the Crops." *NEA Journal* 47:170-72; March 1958.
Insights into the problems faced by migrant children and how some teachers meet these problems.

WOOD, HELEN COWAN. "Teachers Are Important to Migrant Children." *Childhood Education* 33:72-76; October 1956.
Develops the viewpoint that the calm, encouraging, and understanding teacher is the key person in the life of the migrant child as he seeks to become a member of his classroom.

D. School Subject Areas

BATHURST, EFFIE G. *How Children Use Arithmetic.* U.S. Department of Health, Education, and Welfare, Office of Education, Bulletin No. 7. Washington, D. C.: Superintendent of Documents, Government Printing Office, 1951. 19 p.

BATHURST, EFFIE G. *Petersburg Builds a Health Program.* U.S. Department of Health, Education, and Welfare, Office of Education, Bulletin No. 9. Washington, D. C.: Superintendent of Documents, 1949. 50 p.

How grade-school children worked with their parents and other interested citizens to make their home town a healthier and better place to live in.

BATHURST, EFFIE G.; BLACKWOOD, PAUL E.; MACKINTOSH, HELEN K.; and SCHNEIDER, ELSA. *The Place of Subjects in the Curriculum.* U.S. Department of Health, Education, and Welfare, Office of Education, Bulletin No. 12. Washington, D. C.: Superintendent of Documents, 1949. 33 p.

An account of what children do in a day in the fourth grade.

BLACKWOOD, PAUL E. *How Children Learn To Think.* U.S. Department of Health, Education, and Welfare, Office of Education, Bulletin No. 10. Washington, D. C.: Superintendent of Documents, Government Printing Office, 1957. 19 p.

Suggestions of teaching methods to encourage good thinking.

BLOUGH, GLENN O., and BLACKWOOD, PAUL E. *Science Teaching in Rural and Small Town Schools.* U.S. Department of Health, Education, and Welfare, Office of Education, Bulletin No. 5. Washington, D. C.: Superintendent of Documents, Government Printing Office, 1949. 55 p.

BLOUGH, GLENN O., and BLACKWOOD, PAUL E. *Teaching Elementary Science—Suggestions for Classroom Teachers.* U.S. Department of Health, Education, and Welfare, Office of Education, Bulletin No. 4. Washington, D. C.: Superintendent of Documents, Government Printing Office, 1948. 40 p.

CRAIG, GERALD S. *Science in Childhood Education.* Practical Suggestions for Teaching, No. 8. New York: Bureau of Publications, Teachers College, Columbia University, 1944. 86 p.

HILL, WILHELMINA, and MACKINTOSH, HELEN K. *How Children Learn About Human Rights.* Department of Health, Education, and Welfare, Office of Education, Bulletin No. 9. Washington, D. C.: Superintendent of Documents, Government Printing Office, 1957. 23 p.

KINGSLEY, M. "An Experiment in Individualized Reading." *Elementary English* 35: 113-18; February 1958.

Describes an individual reading program for sixth-grade children in which library books are selected on the basis of interest and reading attainment levels.

MACKINTOSH, HELEN K. *How Children Learn To Read.* U.S. Department of Health, Education, and Welfare, Office of Education, Bulletin No. 7. Washington, D. C.: Superintendent of Documents, Government Printing Office, 1954. 16 p.

MACKINTOSH, HELEN K., and HILL, WILHEMINA. *How Children Learn To Write.* U.S. Department of Health, Education, and Welfare, Office of Education, Bulletin No. 2. Washington, D. C.: Superintendent of Documents, Government Printing Office, 1957. 24 p.

SCHNEIDER, ELSA, editor. *Physical Education in Small Schools.* Rev. ed. Department of Rural Education and American Association for Health, Physical Education, and Recreation. Washington, D. C.: National Education Association, 1957. 158 p.

SWENSON, ESTHER J., chairman. *A Look at Continuity in the School Program.* 1958 Yearbook. Washington, D. C.: Association for Supervision and Curriculum Development, National Education Association, 1941. 89 p.

Based on a study of the experiences of 3000 children. Chapter II, "Helping Children Adjust to a New School Community," includes a brief section on migrant children.

WOFFORD, KATE V., editor. *Child Development and Tool Subjects in Rural Areas.* 1941 Yearbook. Washington, D. C.: National Education Association, Department of Rural Education, 1941. 89 p.

Chapters on reading, language arts, and arithmetic, in addition to a general discussion on the tool subjects.

—Cover map, reproduced by permission of American
Automobile Association

—U.S. map from U.S. Department of Health, Education, and
Welfare and U.S. Department of Labor